Designs for
American Gardens

BURPEE®
Designs for American Gardens

Alice Recknagel Ireys

PRENTICE HALL GARDENING

New York   London   Toronto   Sydney   Tokyo   Singapore

PRENTICE HALL GENERAL REFERENCE
15 Columbus Circle
New York, NY 10023

Copyright © 1991 by Alice Recknagel Ireys

Library of Congress Cataloging-in-Publication Data

Ireys, Alice Recknagel.
    Designs for American gardens / Alice Recknagel Ireys.
        p.   cm.
    Includes bibliographical references (p.   ) and index.
    ISBN 0-13-183666-8 (hardcover)
    1. Gardens—Designs and plans.   2. Gardens—United States—Designs
and plans.   I. Title.
    SB473.I7   1991
    712—dc20   91-3664
                                                                  CIP

Designed by Frederick J. Latasa

Manufactured in the United States of America

10   9   8   7   6   5   4   3   2   1

First Edition

To Catherine, Anne and Henry, and my five grandsons Mathew, Stephen, Paul, Nicholas and Alexander.

Acknowledgments

I would like to express my thanks to the many clients whose homes are shown here. They have always been so interested in the progress of their gardens, and it has been a joy to work with them.

To Sandra Ross, George Salley and Bill Elliott for their help on this book I am deeply grateful.

Grateful acknowledgment is also given to the following individuals/organizations for permission to use their works: Molly Adams, Suzanne Bales, Blakeslee/Lane, Cynthia Buff, Connie Cross, Jim Cross, Judy Ferenbach, Mary Franklin, Jane Hoar, Gordon Jones, J. Knapp, Peter Paul Muller, Jr., Planting Fields Arboretum and Allen Rokach.

CONTENTS

Part IV ❧ Five to Ten Acres

Part V ❧ Ten Acres and More

Part VI ❧ Some of My Favorite Plantings

INTRODUCTION

In this book I want to share with you the pleasures that I have had in making the good earth a bit more attractive than it was when the planning began for these country gardens. I hope you will gain some help in developing your own garden, for the joys of creating and caring for a garden, and seeing it mature, are among the greatest pleasures in this world.

My love of gardens dates back to my childhood when I summered on my grandfather's farm in Massachusetts. He taught me how to plant seeds, spacing them just so, providing the little plants with the care they needed, feeling the excitement of watching them grow and then picking a bouquet. I decided then I wanted to pursue a career that involved working with plants.

Making a list of the available opportunities, I settled on landscape architecture. The Cambridge School, a graduate school at Harvard, gave me the education I needed for this career. In the summer months, I worked in a small nursery with Warren Manning, a well-known horticulturist and landscape architect of the early 20th century. This experience added to my knowledge of plants and how they grow. My first job for a landscape architect after graduation was working on a housing project (which paid me $3 a day!). Weekends I spent studying plants at the Brooklyn Botanic Garden—a wonderful place to visit and observe. My second job, with Charles N. Lowrie, a founder of the American Society of Landscape Architects, included both large public projects and private residential properties. That job ended abruptly when he died in 1939, but I continued his office and have been in private practice since then, planning parks, playgrounds and public and private gardens.

Occasionally people ask me if a plan is really necessary. My answer is always the same: yes. Making a garden is a design process. Collecting all the facts about a property, analyzing them and working out a solution give one a chance to study what is really needed.

In the consulting I have done for many gardens, large and small alike, I have always found that it is important to observe existing conditions carefully and to analyze what is good and what needs to be improved. The path to the front door should be lovely and wide, and well planted for year-'round beauty. I then notice how one enters the garden areas. From there, the particular requirements of each homeowner help to determine how the garden will develop.

Garden spaces can be thought of as garden rooms. They can vary in size, and each garden room should have a special use and a special feeling. How you plan to use your garden room makes a great deal of difference in how the design should be carried out. Keep in mind that there should be easy access, good enclosure, an adequate garden floor and a focal point of special interest. A young couple may want space for children to play; an older couple might like a garden filled with unusual plants that incorporates some of the treasures brought back from their travels; people who work at home may prefer a pattern garden that they can see from their window. A successful garden must be in harmony with the house, and there must be harmony between the owners' needs and the design for their garden too.

What do you want in your garden room? You will not be able to include everything, so it is a matter of setting your priorities and planning, just as you would with each room inside the house. When there are a series of garden rooms it is possible to have each one be completely different. If there are teenagers, you may need space for cookouts. If you are a dog fancier, you may want an area for your dog to run. Will your garden room be a place to entertain friends? Are you hoping to grow flowers? The garden rooms in this book have not only different plants but different construction elements such as pavings and hedges; lighting can also increase the effect and pleasure of a garden room. As you read through this book you will find many different garden rooms for inspiration, and perhaps you will find one to include in your own landscape design.

Scale, proportion and unity must be considered in the planning process. If you bear these design elements in mind, you will better be able to imagine and visualize what can be accomplished. Here are the important things to consider:

Scale. Scale is the relative size of an object as it relates to a human being. Scale outdoors is treated quite differently from scale indoors because there are no confining walls or ceilings. One of the most important ways this difference shows up is in the dimensions of outside steps, which have wider treads and lower risers than those in the house. They are more generous because spaces outdoors are so much larger. If a space is divided into units that are skillfully related and arranged, it will seem larger. Different levels create an impression of greater space. I like to raise plant beds above and around a small paved section. The edges of the beds, if high enough, can serve as sitting walls and increase seating capacity of the garden.

Proportion, Balance and Rhythm. These must also be considered in your design. Proportion, a principle that is applied in all arts, requires a pleasing relationship of one part to every other so that the whole composition is comfortable and harmonious. Along with proper proportion in a garden I also consider balance, because this helps to give a garden stability. Balance tends to revolve around a central line, which in a garden is often called an "axis." An axis is a line of vision that can be marked by a panel of grass, a path, a perennial border or a line of trees or shrubs. There are two kinds of balance. Symmetrical balance occurs when elements are arranged evenly on either side of a central feature, be it a door, a fountain, a piece of sculpture or a view. Asymmetrical balance is quite different. With plants, it might involve offsetting a tall group of plants with something that is low spreading, for example. Rhythm, which can be accomplished by the repetition of certain plants, gives a sense of movement in a garden.

Unity and Focal Point. Unity is the ultimate aim of any landscape design. It means having a garden look interesting and at ease and is achieved by a harmonious combination of materials. A focal point is a necessary accent to your garden. Something architectural such as a fountain, pool, bench or sculpture may become the focal point of a garden plan.

There are 14 different properties shown in the pages that follow, all located in USDA Zone 7, but each with different site conditions and size. They show elements of garden design, which involves the overall scheme, and planting design, which is selecting the right plant for each section of the garden. In addition to the first 14 chapters, I have added 3 chapters on plants—trees, shade-loving shrubs and flower combinations. These chapters may be helpful to you when selecting plants for your own property. Some of these plants have been featured in earlier chapters, and some are used in other gardens altogether. Obtaining the right plant for each location takes knowledge of plant material and availability; at the end of this book you will find a list of sources that can help you with this.

If you are interested in planning your own garden, you should begin by acquiring some basic knowledge of plants—what soil conditions they need, when they flower and how they look and grow. Any botanic garden can help you learn these things. What a feeling of contentment comes with planting a garden and watching it grow! The delight in seeing it mature is worth all the work involved, particularly if you planned and planted it yourself.

PART I

One-Half Acre

This border adjacent to a terrace shows June-blooming plants—coralbells, poppies, colum-bine, allium and lavender. Many of these flowers will continue blooming into July.

CHAPTER 1

Gardens for an Attached House

My friends, with whom I have worked for many years, had reached the stage in life when they wanted to scale down to a smaller house with less upkeep both indoors and out. On Long Island they found a cluster-zoned community planned by Innocenti and Webel that consists of 40 acres with a series of individual attached houses, surrounded by open areas of common land. These attached houses are like many of the condominiums being built in the suburbs throughout the country. In most of them the grounds are cared for by the management, but in this particular one the owners are allowed to plan and plant their property themselves. The house they selected on a ½ acre is adjacent to a wildlife sanctuary—an enchanting natural background with old, majestic trees and the occasional added enjoyment of a hoot owl or a handsome red fox prowling the woodsy underbrush.

They were leaving a particularly charming old home with gardens and a greenhouse, and wanted the landscape plan for their new home to incorporate many of the shrubs and plants that had been propagated and nurtured in their previous garden. Continuous bloom from early spring to late fall was considered carefully, and I added evergreens too, so now this really is a garden for all seasons.

If you have plants you love, and hate the idea of leaving them behind, it is easy to relocate them, provided you meet certain conditions. Ideally, plants should be moved before the property is offered for sale. If that isn't possible, contractual arrangements are made between the seller and the buyer for the appropriate replacement of

The summer flower border with annuals of Coreopsis verticillata *'Moonbeam', white salvia and cleome provides season-long color.*

A picket fence with several varieties of roses encloses the garden through which one approaches the front door. On the right is Rosa *'Charles Austin', a hybrid musk that blooms throughout the summer. 'Buff Beauty', another hybrid musk, is on the left.*

plants being removed from the property. In the case of my friends, they established a small nursery on their property several years before moving, where they nurtured cuttings from favorite plants and placed other plants and shrubs they wanted to take along with them. This made for an easy transition when moving day came.

The front entrance has a picket fence and a mixture of roses — old-fashioned shrubs and climbers. The roses were selected for fragrance and continuous bloom, all in varying shades of yellow, peach and pink. 'Golden Wings', 'Buff Beauty', 'Cornelia', 'Charles Austin', 'September Song' and 'Shot Silk' are the old roses; the only modern one that was added is 'Bonica', one of the owners' favorites — a truly everblooming, clear pink shrub (list 1).

As one approaches the front door, the Chinese dogwood (*Cornus Kousa Chinensis*) is lovely in June, with its big white blossoms, and again in the fall, with fruits that look like strawberries. (This dogwood is starting to take the place of the American dogwood, because it is disease-free.) Another tree has recently been added by my client — a Katsura tree (*Cercidiphyllum japonicum*). It is surrounded by 'Blue Boy' and 'Blue Girl' hollies (*Ilex × Meserveae*) with pachysandra as a groundcover. The Katsura has excellent heart-shaped foliage and strong fall color and is disease-free. These two trees each give a distinct seasonal display, the Chinese dogwood in June and the Katsura in the fall (list 1).

Above: *In this small pattern garden dwarf 'Kingsville' boxwood outlines each section. Four of these sections are filled with sweet alyssum, four with buckwheat hulls. A topiary in the center is made from boxwood trained by the owner. In the foreground at the corner of the porch is a container filled with scented geraniums.*

Left: Clematis *'Silver Moon' winds around a post on the entrance porch and will eventually grow all the way to the top.*

Beside the entrance path and beneath the kitchen window is a small pattern garden. This is planted with dwarf 'Kingsville' boxwood (*Buxus microphylla* 'Kingsville') and centered by a taller topiary boxwood (*B. sempervirens* 'Suffruticosa'), both started from cuttings that were brought from the previous house. The dwarf 'Kingsville' is a slow-growing boxwood that needs minimal trimming (once a year). Sweet alyssum adds fragrance in the triangular sections between the boxwoods. For mulch, buckwheat hulls give a nice fine texture to this tiny (12 × 15 feet) garden (list 1).

There is a large Italian terra-cotta container by the front porch overflowing with scented geraniums (*Pelargonium*, in variety) and heliotrope. Clematis climbs up the porch posts: *C.* 'Henryi' with its large white blossoms, soft pink 'Dawn' and 'Silver Moon' with its iridescent lavender flowers. Clematis likes moist shade at its feet. Plant groundcovers like pachysandra or myrtle to shade its roots.

The living room opens onto a brick and flagstone terrace

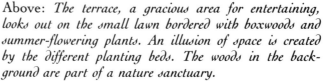

Above: *The terrace, a gracious area for entertaining, looks out on the small lawn bordered with boxwoods and summer-flowering plants. An illusion of space is created by the different planting beds. The woods in the background are part of a nature sanctuary.*

Left: *This small statue is the focal point at the end of the path and is surrounded by lilies and heliotropes, which give a lovely fragrance.*

overlooking the garden. This main section of the garden seems much larger than it really is (only 80 × 90 feet), because it has been divided into six different beds. The owners wanted a great variety of low-growing shrubs and perennials that grow and look well together, and these beds provide a natural place for such groupings of companion plants. The beds are arranged around a central lawn that is bordered by a low evergreen hedge of boxwood (*B. microphylla* 'Kingsville'). Adjacent to the boxwood hedge are a small lead pool and wide borders filled with shrubs, interesting perennials and annuals that provide a succession of bloom from April through November. A charming lead statue stands among the perennials and looks out on these continually blooming plants. These six beds have given my friend a wonderful chance to enjoy the many plants that she loves (lists 2–7).

This garden has taken three years to become really established and now, in fact, there is little need to add anything more. Having reached maturity, these plants require very little attention, making this a low-maintenance garden.

Indoors, the garden room, which is a place for winter flowers, looks out to a different view. A Japanese Zelkova tree (*Zelkova serrata*) shades the glass walls in summer and allows for plenty of sun in the winter; the zelkova is a good substitute for the disease-ridden American elm. Houseplants flourish in the garden room throughout the winter, and then in summer they are put out on the terrace. There is a particularly nice display of topiary herbs made by the owner.

Many of the plants from the former gardens have been included in this small space that provides the pleasure that the owners had wanted. Spring bulbs, summer flowers and colorful fall foliage combined with interesting structure in the garden beds give these clients a year-'round garden.

❧ PLANT LIST

LIST 1 ❧ ENTRANCE PLANTING

Roses

Old-fashioned: 'Buff Beauty', 'Charles Austin', 'Cornelia', 'Golden Wings', 'September Song', 'Shot Silk'

Modern: 'Bonica'

Trees

Cercidiphyllum japonicum (Katsura tree)

Cornus Kousa Chinensis (Chinese dogwood)

Shrubs

Ilex ×Meserveae 'Blue Boy' (Blue holly)

Ilex ×Meserveae 'Blue Girl' (Blue holly)

Pattern Garden

Buxus microphylla 'Kingsville' (Dwarf boxwood)

Buxus sempervirens 'Suffruticosa' (Boxwood)

Lobularia maritima (Sweet alyssum)

LIST 2 ❧ LEFT GARDEN BORDER

Perennials

Aquilegia Hybrid 'McKana's Giant' (Columbine)

Coreopsis verticillata 'Moonbeam' (Tickseed, Coreopsis)

Echinops exaltatus (Globe thistle)

Epimedium ×rubrum (Bishop's cap)

Heuchera sanguinea (Coralbells)

Lavandula angustifolia 'Munstead' (Lavender)

Lilium ×aurelianense 'Pink Perfection' (Lily)

Nepeta Mussinii (Catmint)

Physostegia virginiana 'Summer Snow' (False dragonhead)

Teucrium Chamaedrys (Germander)

Thymus pseudolanginosus (Woolly thyme)

Tricyrtis hirta (Toad lily)

Veronica longifolia (Speedwell)

Annuals

Antirrhinum (Snapdragons)

Impatiens (Impatiens)

Nicotiana (Flowering tobacco)

LIST 3 ❧ RIGHT GARDEN BORDER

Perennials

Achillea Ptarmica 'The Pearl' (Yarrow)

Allium caeruleum (Flowering onion)

Aquilegia flabellata 'Alba' (Columbine)

Aquilegia Hybrid 'McKana's Giant' (Columbine)

Aster novi-belgii 'Professor Kippenburg' (Aster)

Coreopsis verticillata 'Moonbeam' (Tickseed, Coreopsis)

Heuchera sanguinea (Coralbells)

Lavandula angustifolia 'Munstead' (Lavender)

Malva Alcea fastigiata (Musk mallow)

Nepeta Mussinii (Catmint)

(continued)

(continued)

Physostegia virginiana 'Summer Snow' (False dragonhead)

Sedum spectabile 'Autumn Joy' (Stonecrop)

Stokesia laevis 'Blue Danube' (Stokes' aster)

Thymus pseudolanginosus (Woolly thyme)

Annuals

Antirrhinum (Snapdragons)

Impatiens (Impatiens)

Nicotiana (Flowering tobacco)

LIST 4 ❧ SHRUB BORDER
Shrubs

Buddleia Davidii 'White Profusion' (Butterfly bush)

Ilex ×aquipernyi 'San Jose' (Holly)

Ilex crenata (Japanese holly)

Ilex ×cornuta 'Nellie R. Stevens' (Holly)

Philadelphus coronarius (Mock orange)

Viburnum Carlesii (Mayflower viburnum)

Perennials

Alchemilla pubescens (Lady's-mantle)

Astilbe ×Arendsii 'Rheinland' (Astilbe)

Hosta Fortunei obscura (Plantain lily)

Hosta lancifolia alba (Plantain lily)

Hosta lancifolia albomarginata (Plantain lily)

Hosta Seiboldiana 'August Moon' (Plantain lily)

Hosta undulata 'Variegata' (Plantain lily)

Lysimachia punctata (Loosestrife)

Teucrium Chamaedrys (Germander)

LIST 5 ❧ AZALEA BORDER

Rhododendron balsaminiflora (Azalea)

Rhododendron 'Satsuki' (Azalea gumpo)

Rhododendron Schlippenbachii (Royal azalea)

Perennials and Bulbs

Anemone japonica 'September Charm' (Anemone)

Astilbe chinensis 'Pumila' (Astilbe)

Clematis Davidiana (Clematis)

Narcissus triandrus 'Moonshine' (Spring miniature bulb)

Nephrolepis exaltata 'Bostoniensis' (Boston fern)

Phlox divaricata (Phlox)

Tulipa Clusiana (Tulip)

LIST 6 ❧ LILAC BORDER
Shrubs

Ilex ×Meserveae 'Blue Prince' (Blue holly)

Ilex ×Meserveae 'Blue Princess' (Blue holly)

Syringa Meyeri 'Palabin' (Dwarf Korean lilac)

Perennials

Astilbe ×Arendsii 'Peach Blossom' (Astilbe)

Heuchera micrantha 'Palace Purple' (Coralbells)

LIST 7 ❧ SHADY BACK BORDER
Shrubs

Ilex crenata (Japanese holly)

Ilex ×Meserveae 'Blue Princess' (Blue holly)

Kerria japonica (Japanese rose)

Leucothoe Fontanesiana (Drooping leucothoe)

Rhododendron 'Robin Hill' (Azalea)

Sarcococca humilis (Sweet box)

Skimmia japonica (Skimmia)

Viburnum tomentosum (Double file viburnum)

Early Spring Bulbs

Anemone blanda (Windflower)

Muscari armeniacum (Grape hyacinth)

Narcissus cyclamineus (Daffodil)

Narcissus cyclamineus 'February Gold' (Daffodil)

Scilla campanulata (Wood hyacinth)

Tulipa Greigii (Tulip)

Tulipa tarda (Tulip)

Groundcovers

Asarum europaeum (European ginger)

Asperula odorata (Sweet woodruff)

Astilbe ×Adrendsii 'Bridal Veil' (Astilbe)

Astilbe ×Adrendsii 'Deutschland' (Astilbe)

Astilbe ×Adrendsii 'Erica' (Astilbe)

Epimedium, in variety (Fireweed; yellow, pink and white)

Hedera Helix 'Pedata' (Bird's foot ivy)

Ferns
Athyrium Filix-femina (Lady fern)
Dryopteris cristata (Crested wood fern)
Osmunda cinnamomea (Cinnamon fern)

Perennials
Hemerocallis 'Emerald Gown' (Daylily)
Hemerocallis 'Madame Bellum' (Daylily)
Hemerocallis 'Mrs. Wyman' (Daylily)

Hemerocallis 'Serene Scene' (Daylily)
Hemerocallis 'Thumbelina' (Daylily)
Hosta crispula (Plantain lily)
Hosta plantaginea 'Grandiflora' (Plantain lily)
Hosta tardiflora (Plantain lily)
Lilium canadense (Wild yellow lily)
Liriope Muscari (Lilyturf)
Primula, in variety (Primrose)

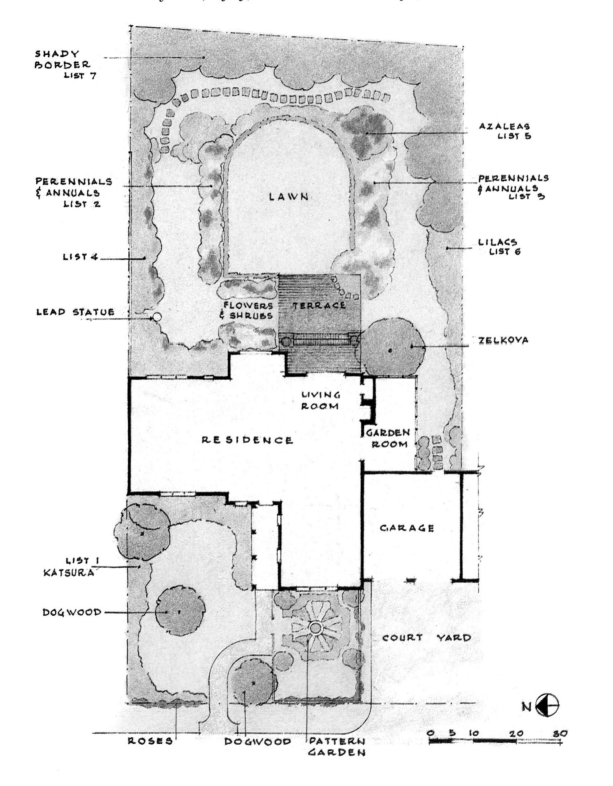

CHAPTER 2

Garden Rooms for a Small House on a Hill

This little old saltbox house situated on a hill caught the eye of a discriminating couple in search of a simple setting for their retirement years. These old friends were moving from a larger house with many gardens. I had worked on several gardens with them before their move, and had looked at many potential properties, so by this point, I knew what they would need. This ½-acre site suited them nicely. They wanted a small terrace for breakfast and a larger one for family gatherings and entertaining. Their other requirements were a perennial garden for favorite plants, a place for roses, a swimming pool and a guesthouse. The sloping site of their new property helped me fit their many requests into a compact plan. The changes in grade gave me a chance to create a series of different spaces, connected by steps where necessary. Having different spaces makes the small garden seem larger. The existing hollies, styrax and old trees made the plan more interesting.

Some of their favorite things were brought from their previous house, which was to be torn down. Beautiful old flagstones were incorporated in the new terrace, and delicate wrought-iron fences were used to frame a view into the garden. Two lovely old carriage lamps were set on each side of the door leading into the dining room.

The curving front steps and ramp make an easy approach. Korean boxwood (*Buxus microphylla koreana*) and abelia (*Abelia*

The breakfast terrace has its own little garden. Here begonias carry out the pink-and-white theme. White perennial candytuft (Iberis sempervirens) is planted along the edge. Clumps of skimmia, a nice evergreen shrub for year-'round effect, fill in above the sitting wall.

Pots of pink and white impatiens line the steps of the dining room entrance. English boxwoods and two dwarf cedars flank the doors.

×*grandiflora*) line the path toward the house. A pair of boxwood (*B. sempervirens*) flank the front door (list 1), and I allowed plenty of space for container plants on this wide terrace. On the street side, Japanese yews (*Taxus cuspidata*) have been encouraged to grow and now, five years later, combined with forsythia, they make a dense screen that hides the view of neighboring houses. That planting has become so dense, in fact, that it has altogether replaced the front lawn (list 2).

Continuing around the house, there is a climbing hydrangea (*Hydrangea petiolaris*) that has grown almost to the top of the chimney. This plant is slow to flower, but once blossoms start, it is a spectacular sight. The June flowers are long-lasting, and the attractive seedpods are held throughout the year. On the right, a small rose garden contains a dozen of the owners' favorite roses for cutting. The colors were selected to coordinate with the beautifully furnished interior of the house (list 3).

Clematis montana rubens *climbs a wrought-iron fence through which the front garden is visible.* Astilbe × Arendsii *'Deutschland' (white) and* Astilbe Hybrid *'Erica' (pink) in the foreground bloom for several weeks.*

Passing through the wrought-iron gates, you come to a large flagstone terrace bordered by a small perennial garden (list 4). From this terrace, three steps lead up to a smaller brick terrace. Here masses of bulbs followed by wax begonias give color from spring until frost. A few unusual plants—*Enkianthus campanulatus* and *Daphne* 'Carol Mackie'—give added interest and fragrance to this area. At the corner of the upper terrace, a weeping 'Red Jade' crab apple (*Malus* 'Red Jade') has spread enough to shade part of the lower terrace as well, creating a comfortable, cool place to sit. Against the building a styrax (*Styrax japonicus*) has been planted, which makes an interesting accent with its mottled bark and lovely white flowers, followed in fall with pale blue berries.

From the lower terrace, a walk leads to the pool. Hollies (*Ilex opaca*) and a star magnolia (*Magnolia stellata*) surround the pool. A long sitting wall holds the hillside away from the lawn, and softens the awkward angle of the property.

Creating a level area for the pool meant that a slope had to be made at the far end of the garden. Euonymus (*Euonymus japonica* 'Manhattan'), jasmine (*Jasminum nudiflorum*) and Baltic ivy (*Hedera Helix* 'Baltica') were planted on this slope. At the bottom, a small

In this view looking toward the house from the pool, the large terrace is on the left and the small breakfast terrace is on the right. A dwarf crab apple (Malus 'Red Jade') spreads its branches over both and provides shade for seating.

wildflower garden draws attention in early spring with trillium, various types of violets and trout lilies. A step ramp leads from the pool to the service area along the back of the guesthouse. (This ramp, a grass path 3 feet wide, has a 6-inch riser every 5 feet.) An espaliered *Euonymus* 'Manhattan' softens the wall and screens the building's exposed foundation.

Across the grass path is a compost area where grass clippings and other garden refuse are layered with soil, to create organic matter that enriches the entire garden. Continuing through an old wooden gate, you come back to the front steps that lead from the parking area to the back door. It was difficult to work out a comfortable plan here, because the space was small and the grade was steep. So in order to get up the nine feet to the back door, I turned the steps three times, providing a nice approach and an unusual series of pockets for plants as well.

The garage situated below the house is framed by two posts set 10 feet out from the building and planted with wisteria (*Wisteria sinensis*). Now the eye is drawn to the wisteria-clad posts rather than the garage doors. The arbor makes a shady spot to park, and is

Wisteria trained on a wooden trellis provides an easy and attractive camouflage for the garage doors. An added benefit is a shady place to park.

lovely and sweet-smelling when in bloom. Wisteria does require a lot of pruning, so be prepared to spend time each month on this chore or your vine will take over. An elevator was added, and to hide this tall, narrow addition, a fleece vine (*Polygonum Aubertii*) was planted. This late summer bloomer can grow up to 40 feet in one season, and the small white flowers make a strong show in August.

A small vegetable garden with lettuce, tomatoes and parsley was planted along the property line until the trees grew and shaded it out. This area is now used as a cutting garden for spring bulbs (list 5). (A spring planting works where a summer one would not, because the trees haven't yet fully leafed-out in spring.) As it is too shady for tulips to rebloom, a new collection is planted each year.

One of the nicest things about this small property is the enjoyment it has given to my clients. I, too, am satisfied as I walk around with my friend and see things that I know she loves. The 'Red Jade' crab apple has made a flowering umbrella that shades her favorite seat; the shiny hollies provide berries for Christmas decorations; the Korean boxwood has billowed over the front steps and the complete enclosure hides the neighbors so it feels like being in the country rather than the suburbs.

PLANT LIST

LIST 1 ◆ FRONT PLANTING ALONG RAMP

Abelia ×*grandiflora* (Abelia)

Buxus microphylla koreana (Korean boxwood)

Buxus sempervirens (Boxwood)

Cornus Kousa Chinensis (Chinese dogwood)

Hedera Helix 'Baltica' (English ivy)

Ilex crenata (Japanese holly)

LIST 2 ◆ FRONT PLANTING ALONG STREET

Cornus Kousa Chinensis (Chinese dogwood)

Forsythia ×*intermedia* (Forsythia)

Ilex ×*Meserveae* 'Blue Boy' (Blue holly)

Taxus cuspidata (Japanese yew)

LIST 3 ◆ ROSES FOR CUTTING

'Eclipse' (yellow)

'First Prize' (pale pink)

'Helen Traubel' (pink)

'Peace' (yellow with pink)

'Queen Elizabeth' (pink)

'Tiffany' (pink)

LIST 4 ◆ SMALL PERENNIAL GARDEN

Anemone japonica 'September Charm' (Anemone)

Aster ×*Frikartii* (Aster)

Astilbe ×*Arendsii* 'Deutschland' (Astilbe)

Astilbe ×*Arendsii* 'Erica' (Astilbe)

Aquilegia chrysantha (Columbine)

Iberis sempervirens (Candytuft)

Iris sibirica 'Lady Godiva' (Siberian iris)

Lupinus polyphyllus (Lupine)

Perovskia atriplicifolia (Russian sage)

Phlox carolina 'Miss Lingard' (Phlox)

Platycodon grandiflorus 'Albus' (Balloon flower)

LIST 5 ◆ SPRING CUTTING GARDEN (BULBS)

Camassia (Camass; blue)

Double *Narcissus* 'Cheerfulness' (Daffodil; white)

Narcissus Pseudonarcissus 'Mt. Hood' (Daffodil; white)

Narcissus triandrus 'Thalia' (Daffodil; white)

Scilla campanulata (Wood hyacinth; blue and white)

Tulipa 'Angelique' (Tulip)

Tulipa 'Clara Butt' (Tulip)

Tulipa 'Apricot Beauty' (Tulip)

Tulipa 'Mt. Tacoma' (Tulip; white)

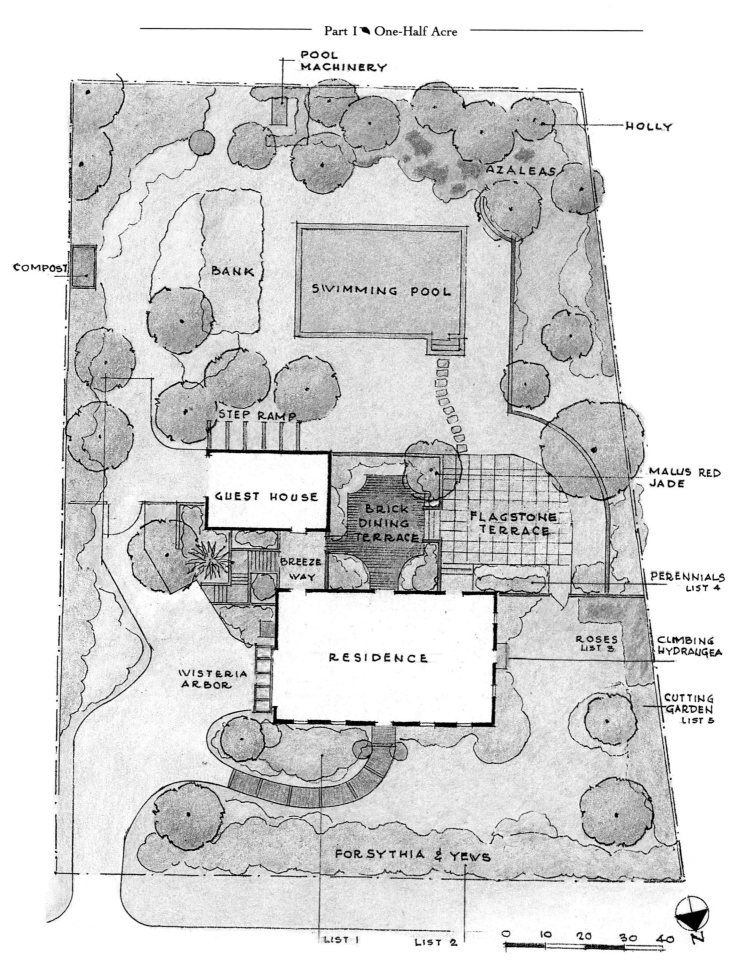

POOL
MACHINERY

HOLLY

AZALEAS

COMPOST

BANK

SWIMMING POOL

STEP RAMP

MALUS RED
JADE

GUEST HOUSE

BRICK
DINING
TERRACE

FLAGSTONE
TERRACE

BREEZE
WAY

PERENNIALS
LIST 4

ROSES
LIST 3

CLIMBING
HYDRANGEA

RESIDENCE

WISTERIA
ARBOR

CUTTING
GARDEN
LIST 5

FORSYTHIA & YEWS

LIST 1

LIST 2

0   10   20   30   40   N

CHAPTER 3

Five Small Gardens Near the Sea

One of my dearest and oldest friends bought this summer cottage 30 years ago. The property is small (only 80 × 150 feet), and it opens on one of Long Island's bays, facing southwest to the prevailing breezes. The basic design of five small, protected gardens has remained over the years. My friend has always wanted annuals, perennials, roses and other plants that will flourish by the sea, and she requires that the garden look neat and trim at all times.

Every room of the house looks out to a small garden, so that no matter where you sit inside there is something lovely to see. The living room is open on two sides. To the south are roses, a Chinese dogwood (*Cornus Kousa Chinensis*) and an annual and perennial border; to the north, a lawn bordered with *Rosa rugosa* and stands of grasses with a view of the bay beyond. This view is especially nice from the large porch. A Japanese black pine (*Pinus Thunbergii*) frames the bedroom window, with bayberry (*Myrica pensylvanica*) below. The bathroom overlooks a little hidden garden; and the dining room, a small enclosed perennial border and birdbath. From the guest room there are three views—to the east a dogwood, to the north a round garden and to the west, a daylily walk.

Two dwarf cypress (*Chamaecyparis obtusa* 'Nana') flank the wide-paved entrance approaching the house from the paved driveway. A Goldenrain tree (*Koelreuteria paniculata*) with its long summer panicles of yellow provides a showy accent for a few weeks in midsummer. On the right, a cheerful flower garden with its mass of

The early June plantings in the garden are visible through the front window.

*Looking through the small rose garden to the front entrance is a view of the Chinese dogwood (*Cornus Kousa Chinensis*) in full bloom. Planted some 30 years ago, it is the dominant feature near the front entrance of this cottage. Its beautiful white flowers in June last for many weeks.* Leucothoe Fontanesiana *is planted beneath the dogwood and acts as a groundcover.*

flowers arranged in a neat and trim fashion sets the tone for the rest of the property. A rose garden (list 1) on the left is set between the front path and the garage. It has a low wall along the walk, so the garden isn't revealed all at once. There are 10 different types of roses in this small space, with the climber 'Blaze' planted to cover the garage wall. The pinks, whites and reds of these roses are a dazzling display each June. Beside the house a handsome Chinese dogwood (*Cornus Kousa Chinensis*), moved from the owner's previous home, has grown extremely well. Combined with an underplanting of leucothoe (*Leucothoe Fontanesiana*), a broad-leafed evergreen, this makes a most interesting planting. The leucothoe is particularly nice for cutting throughout the year.

The main flower garden (list 2) is opposite the front door and living room window. It is 10 × 20 feet, and planned to be colorful from June until late fall. Perennial white phlox, *Buddleia, Lythrum* and Shasta and Montauk daisies form the background for an assortment of annuals—sweet alyssum, blue ageratum, blue salvia and pink geraniums. Annuals are excellent summer-bloomers and help carry the perennial plants through the summer months. It is interesting to note that this garden changes every week when the various perennials come into bloom and the annuals develop more fully.

As we continue on the walk that curves around the west of the house toward the bay, we notice two Russian olives (*Elaeagnus angustifolia*) that have grown together, creating a beautiful archway. Just to the right of the walk, they arch over a circular garden (list 3) bordered with box-leaved hollies (*Ilex crenata* 'Convexa') and Douglas firs (*Pseudotsuga Menziesii*). As the Douglas firs have matured, *Hydrangea macrophylla* 'Maressii' have been added to bring summer bloom into an otherwise green garden. A grass path bordered with daylilies leads to an enclosed garden (list 4) that is only 300 square feet. This tiny garden with its simple board fence has a brick-paved area that is edged with boxwood (*Buxus sempervirens*) and is just large enough for two chairs. It makes a charming place for relaxing out of the wind and observing the birds in the little birdbath that is centered opposite the dining room window. Below this window hostas (*Hosta crispula*) bloom for a long time, about six weeks in the summer. *Clethra* planted in one corner sends it fragrance into the dining room. Behind the boxwood hedge are gas plants (*Dictamnus*), phlox (*Phlox carolina* 'Miss Lingard'), yellow *Lysimachia punctata*,

This sun-drenched walkway is actually part of the tiny garden (14 × 22 feet) hidden at the right. Behind the boxwood border, white gas plant and goatsbeard are in bloom against the fence.

Montauk daisies and butterfly weed (*Asclepias tuberosa*). Beyond the fence is a 9-foot privet hedge (*Ligustrum amurense*), and blue morning glories are planted here every year to climb the privet. It's fun to count how many flowers there are each morning on this lovely climbing vine.

There is another little hidden terrace passing through the second gate with the view of the water. For many years the branches of a Japanese black pine shaded this tiny space but, like many of the Japanese black pines on Long Island, the old tree succumbed to disease. A group of native red cedar (*Juniperus virginiana*) was substituted. The tops of the cedars were removed to encourage them to grow horizontally and echo the low lines of the house. Montauk daisies bring color to this terrace in October. *Lythrum* has also thrived in this contained space. Its pink spiky flowers are stunning against the clear blue water.

Small beds of grasses (list 5) flank the steps to the beach, creating a focal point when viewed from the living room doorway. Although grasses have never been my favorite plants, here by the water they look as if they really belong. Contrary to popular opinion, I find grasses are difficult to use in many places. They are not easy to combine or control effectively, and they are often apt to look scraggly.

In this detail of the grasses planted on each side of the entrance to the beach, Artemisia ludoviciana 'Silver Mound' *is backed by* Helictotrichon sempervirens *and* Sesleria autumnalis. Rosa rugosa *grows at the top of the bank behind the brick wall.*

The owner stands in front of her summer flower garden with its edging of sweet alyssum and geraniums. Blue salvia, artemisia and cleome give continuous summer bloom.

This seaside garden is the fourth one that my friend and I have planned and planted together over the years. We share a love of gardening, and work very well together. She turned to me for help with planning, primarily; I left many of the decisions about planting to her. As often happens, the basic bones of the garden have remained fairly constant, while some of the plants have changed. It is interesting to note the particular plants that have done extremely well over this long period of time—*Rosa rugosa*, juniper, *Pyracantha*, Douglas fir, privet and Russian olive.

The advantage of working with a client over a long period of time is that together, we can make changes and enjoy the results. It has given me pleasure through the years to see her removing every deadhead in the rose garden and pinching back the perennials. She even enjoys sweeping the little path so that not a single leaf remains. She is a true lover of her garden.

Nowadays she describes her work in the garden this way: "At 97 I have orders not to remove any deadheads, for often when I did I fell after them. Although I never hurt myself badly, I found lying in my flowers and waiting for someone to pick me up is a waste of time. So my young housekeeper is the gardener, and I am the housekeeper. The house likes it and the garden looks better too, so all is well with my beloved home, 'Windsong.' "

PLANT LIST

LIST 1 ❧ ROSE GARDEN

'Blaze' (on garage)
'Eclipse'
'First Prize'
'Helen Traubel'
'John F. Kennedy'
'Peace'
'Queen Elizabeth'
'Royal Highness'
'Talisman'
'Tiffany'
'Touch of Class'

LIST 2 ❧ FLOWER GARDEN

Perennials

Astilbe ×Adrensii 'Deutschland' (Astilbe)
Daisies (Shasta and Montauk)
Digitalis purpurea (Foxglove)
Lythrum virgatum 'Morden Pink'
  (Loosestrife)
Phlox carolina 'Miss Lingard' (Phlox)

Annuals—change each year

Ageratum (Ageratum)
Dahlia (Dahlias)
Lobularia maritima (Sweet alyssum)
Pelargonium (Geraniums)
Salvia (Blue salvia)

Shrubs

Buddleia Davidii 'Snow Bank' (Butterfly
  bush)

LIST 3 ❧ CIRCULAR GARDEN

Berberis ×mentorensis (Mentor barberry)
Elaeagnus angustifolia (Russian olive)
Hydrangea macrophylla 'Maressii'
  (Hydrangea)
Ilex crenata 'Convexa' (Holly)
Pseudotsuga Menziesii (Douglas fir)
Viburnum tomentosum (Double file
  viburnum)

LIST 4 ❧ ENCLOSED GARDEN

Aruncus dioicus (Goatsbeard)
Asclepias tuberosa (Butterfly weed)
Buddleia Davidii 'Empire Blue' (Butterfly
  bush)
Buxus sempervirens (Boxwood)
Clethra alnifolia (Summer-sweet)
Dictamnus albus (Gas plant)
Hosta lancifolia (Plantain lily)
Sedum spectabile 'Autumn Joy' (Stonecrop)

LIST 5 ❧ GRASSES

Artemisia Schmidtiana 'Silver Mound'
  (Mugwort)
Helictotrichon sempervirens
Sesleria autumnalis

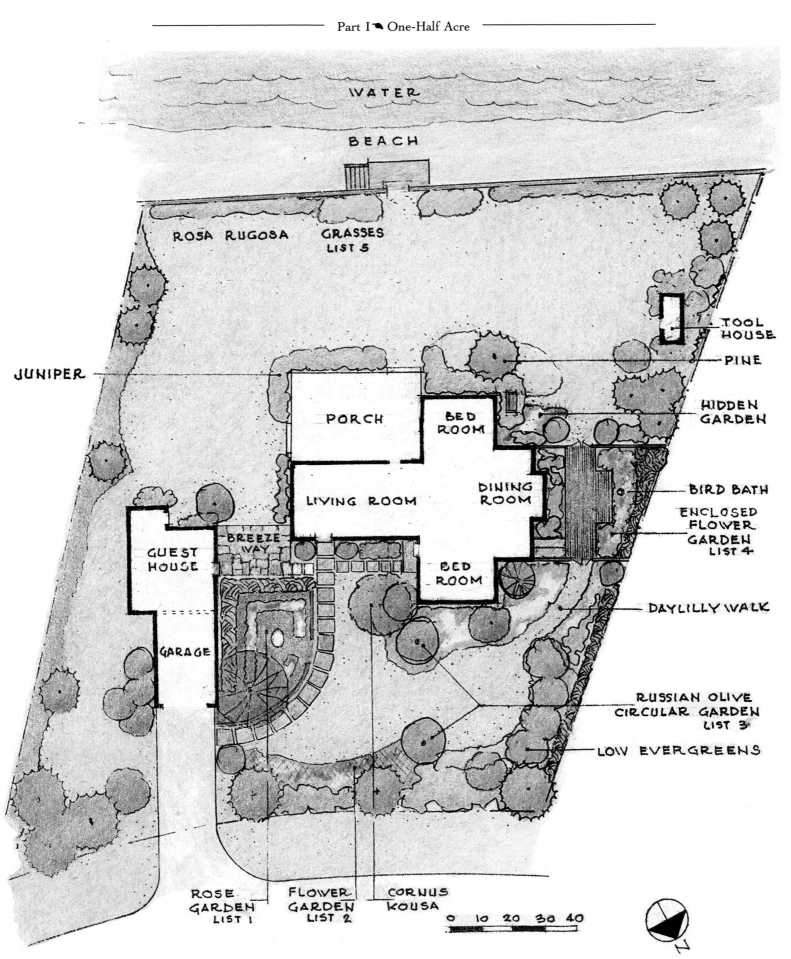

WATER

BEACH

ROSA RUGOSA   GRASSES
               LIST 5

JUNIPER

PORCH   BED
               ROOM

TOOL
HOUSE

PINE

HIDDEN
GARDEN

LIVING ROOM   DINING
               ROOM

BIRD BATH

ENCLOSED
FLOWER
GARDEN
LIST 4

GUEST
HOUSE

BREEZE
WAY

BED
ROOM

DAYLILLY WALK

GARAGE

RUSSIAN OLIVE
CIRCULAR GARDEN
LIST 3

LOW EVERGREENS

ROSE   FLOWER   CORNUS
GARDEN   GARDEN   KOUSA
LIST 1   LIST 2

0 10 20 30 40

N

PART II

One to Two Acres

The entrance into this garden shows potted plants of begonias, chrysanthemums and cranesbill that give continuous bloom throughout the summer. In the garden phlox, yarrow, asters, dianthus, catmint, butterfly weed and globe thistle bloom in July and August.

CHAPTER 4

A Summer Home by a Bay with Many Gardens

This small cottage, on one acre of land with absolutely no planting when purchased, has been added on to over the years, and the surrounding space developed into interesting summer gardens. The owner, a long-time friend, enjoys doing much of the gardening herself and is very knowledgeable about plants. She works hard to achieve continuous bloom throughout the summer months on this seashore property. The flat property overlooks the bay and had not a single tree when we started some 15 years ago. Fortunately, the client loved her open view. It was framed originally with some Japanese black pines (*Pinus Thunbergii*), but about 20 years ago they began to die off from the fungus cenangium canker, and infestations of turpentine beetles, pinewood nematodes and the pine sawfly. The trees were replaced with Russian olives (*Elaeagnus angustifolia*). Around the house I provided a series of sheltered spots suitable for growing flowers.

The front door is approached by a walk through a perennial border (list 1). The flowers include iris, phlox, geraniums, globe thistles and lilies selected for their long season of bloom. The edging along the walk includes perennial candytuft, coralbells and perennial geraniums. An espaliered viburnum (*Viburnum tomentosum*) grows by the front door, and beyond it, the path leads to a little hidden terrace set into a protected corner. Vines are planted on trellises next to the house—honeysuckle (*Lonicera Heckrottii*) and *Clematis* (*C. montana rubens*). Pots of geraniums add lots of color to this spot.

Looking back at the house from the street the shape of the hawthorn tree adds interest, and the perennial border on the left is in June bloom.

A perennial border is planted along the curved walk from the driveway to the front door. In June the globe thistle, yellow lilies and blue salvias bloom along with the pink geraniums and pale yellow marigolds. The Goldenrain tree (Koelreuteria) at the end of the path blooms in the summer with pale yellow flowers followed by balloonlike seedpods. Plantings against the house consist of abelias and dwarf azaleas.

On the right-hand side of the path there is an island of inkberry (*Ilex glabra*) and abelia (*Abelia* ×*grandiflora*), which directs your eye to the far end of the property. Here behind a little bench is a stand of my favorite hollies, *Ilex* ×*altaclarensis* 'Camelliifolia'. These have done extremely well in this seashore environment. Farther to the right, along the road, climbing yellow roses ('Golden Showers') on a post-and-rail fence make a good screen for passing traffic. This rose has large yellow flowers on and off all season, and the large glossy leaves are very attractive. Also planted along this fence are flowering shrubs, hollies and one lovely cedar (*Cedrus atlantica* 'Glauca') that has done extremely well. The flowering shrubs include *Viburnum tomentosum*, *Abelia* ×*grandiflora*, *Hypericum* and *Tamarix*.

Around the house, the view opens onto a swimming pool surrounded by a post-and-rail fence covered with climbing apricot trumpet vine (*Campsis* ×*Tagliabuana* 'Madame Galen'). Russian olives (*Elaeagnus angustifolia*) and a few healthy old Japanese black pines (*Pinus Thunbergii*) grow in this exposed, windy part of the garden, providing some protection for the pool. The edge of the pool is surrounded by junipers (*Juniperus horizontalis* 'Blue Rug'), which soften the lines with a lovely gray-green color.

In this exposed, windy place I have tried cherries, locusts, pin oaks and sycamores, hoping they would give some shade to this hot, dry area. They did not die, but grew smaller and smaller until finally they had to be removed. One cherry tree is left, which gives a few blossoms and very little shade in summer.

The daylily border is a mass of color throughout July and August. The varieties shown here are 'Mary Todd', 'Primrose Frills' and 'Southern Pride'. The Rosa rugosa *behind the daylilies has finished blooming, but the Russian olive with its silver foliage is still interesting.*

A covered porch and terrace extend from the living room toward the bay. To the left is a wide border of daylilies (list 2) with many different varieties that bloom from June to September, in colors ranging from soft yellow to deep orange. When selecting daylilies, first consider the color you want, then the height, using the taller varieties at the back and the shorter in front. Next consider the seasons of bloom, generally designated as "early," "midseason" and "late." In this garden, daylilies are planted close together to cut down on weeding, in front of a staggered hedgerow of Russian olives. *Rosa rugosa* fills the space between the daylilies and the gray-leaved olives. The deep pink blooms of the *Rosa rugosa* provide interest before the daylilies flower. This border of daylilies has been in place for 10 years, and at the edge of the border some of the older plants have been removed and 'Stella d'Oro' and 'Eenie Weenie' have been added—good low-growing varieties that are continuous bloomers. It is a joy to see the daylilies burst into glorious flower year after year.

Adjacent to the garage on the east side is a rose garden (list 3) with four raised railroad-tie beds. Each bed contains eight roses and an edging of sweet alyssum, which adds fragrance throughout the summer. Pears are espaliered against the garage wall. Farther around the house, a small cutting garden (list 4) filled with lilies, zinnias, snapdragons and dahlias is protected from rabbits and woodchucks by a rustic picket fence.

The library window looks out to a protected spot with a birch

tree (*Betula pendula* 'Youngii') growing alongside a small water basin and a statue of St. Francis. Blueberry bushes (*Vaccinium corymbosum*) enclose this little garden (list 5).

We have ended up with an open, rambling plan that provides an opportunity to grow many of the flowers that thrive near the sea.

A corner of the rose garden shows the raised bed with sweet alyssum edging. 'French Lace' and 'Spartan' are two of the roses featured here.

Left: *This cutting garden has a narrow path of pavers making it easy to pick the lilies, snapdragons, dahlias, zinnias and cosmos.*

PLANT LIST

LIST 1 🐦 PERENNIAL BORDER

Aconitum Fischeri (Monkshood)

Aquilegia Hybrids (Columbine)

Chrysanthemum maximum 'Alaska' (Chrysanthemum; early)

Chrysanthemum maximum 'Marconi' (Chrysanthemum; midseason)

Chrysanthemum maximum 'Victor' (Chrysanthemum; late)

Digitalis purpurea (Foxglove)

Echinops exaltatus (Globe thistle)

Heuchera sanguinea (Coralbells)

Iris germanica 'Canary Cadence' (German iris)

Iris germanica 'Night Deposit' (German iris)

Lilium auratum (Goldbond lily; in August)

Lilium candidum (Madonna lily; in June)

Lilium regale (Regal lily; in July)

Phlox carolina 'Miss Lingard' (Phlox)

Phlox decussata 'White Admiral' (Phlox)

Sanguineum 'Album' (Perennial geranium)

LIST 2 🐦 DAYLILY BORDER (*Hemerocallis*)

'Beloved Country'

'Eenie Weenie'

'Hyperion'

'Jake Russell'

'Lemona'

'Mary Todd'

'Mrs. Wyman'

'Primrose Frills'

'Southern Pride'

'Stella d'Oro'

LIST 3 🐦 ROSE GARDEN

'Apricot Nectar'

'French Lace'

Lobularia maritima (Sweet alyssum; as a border plant)

'Red Gold'

'Spartan'

LIST 4 🐦 SMALL CUTTING GARDEN

Antirrhinum (Snapdragons; yellow)

Cosmos (Cosmos; yellow and pink)

Dahlia (Dahlias; peach)

Lilium 'Connecticut King' (Lily; yellow)

Lilium 'Mount Everest' (Lily; white)

Lilium 'Sterling Star' (Lily; white)

Zinnia (Zinnia; yellow)

LIST 5 🐦 LIBRARY GARDEN

Betula pendula 'Youngii' (Weeping birch)

Hosta undulata 'Variegata' (Plantain lily; white)

Impatiens (Impatiens; white)

Vaccinium corymbosum (Blueberry)

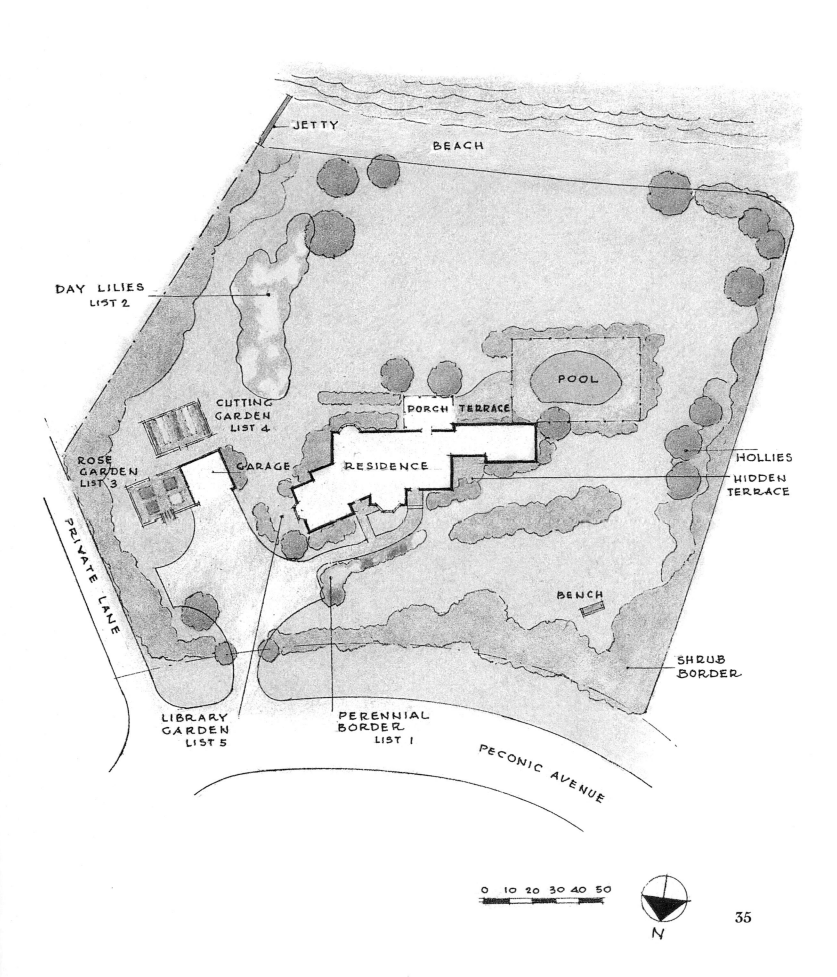

JETTY

BEACH

DAY LILIES
LIST 2

POOL

CUTTING
GARDEN
LIST 4

PORCH TERRACE

ROSE
GARDEN
LIST 3

GARAGE

RESIDENCE

HOLLIES

HIDDEN
TERRACE

PRIVATE LANE

BENCH

SHRUB
BORDER

LIBRARY
GARDEN
LIST 5

PERENNIAL
BORDER
LIST 1

PECONIC AVENUE

0 10 20 30 40 50

N

CHAPTER 5

An Old Cape Cod House with a Cottage Garden

The oldest house in Quogue, Long Island, was built around 1730 as a shepherd's cottage. Altered in 1790 to a Cape Cod-style house, it is now a weekend retreat. I first met the owners eight years ago after they had restored the cottage from a tumble-down state and were ready to focus on the grounds surrounding it, a little over an acre. They had seen my gardens around other houses and asked me to help them.

True to the 18th-century tradition for a small country home, the plantings surrounding the house and barn have been kept very simple. The house faces a heavily traveled road that needed to be screened. With a massive planting of pines, hollies, spruce, rhodo-dendron and viburnum on a wide berm, the little cottage is now completely hidden (list 1). A berm is an earth mound used for special effects. Here it was necessary to create a barrier, varying in height from four to six feet, from the noisy road. Instead of using extensive foundation planting (which I felt wouldn't suit such an old house), we chose to plant a clump of common white lilacs (*Syringa vulgaris*) at one corner of the cottage, and a pair of boxwood (*Buxus sempervirens* 'Suffruticosa') at the front door. A brick path leads from the parking area to this entrance. It leads past a bell hung on a high post, which serves as an effective way of announcing arriving guests. On the opposite side of the parking area a row of old-fashioned cedar, dogwood and rhododendron were added for additional privacy.

One of our first projects was the addition of a brick terrace

Achillea Hybrid 'Moonshine' lends a spot of color outside the pool changing rooms. This will bloom all summer.

The planting at the front door intentionally imitates the simple style of the early 18th century. Two English boxwoods flank the door.

close to the kitchen. A Bradford pear (*Pyrus Calleryana* 'Bradford') was planted in the center to give afternoon shade. This tree has lovely spring flowers, stunning autumn color and inconspicuous pears.

From this terrace a beautiful flower border (list 2)—the owner's interpretation of an English cottage garden—leads to a crab-apple allée (*Malus floribunda*). Cottage gardens historically were not formally planned. People planted flowers that they liked and knew would do well. In this garden the owners have planted their favorite old-fashioned flowers: hollyhocks, dianthus, lupines, peonies, astilbes and phlox. Summer-flowering shrubs have been added as well, together with herbs, grasses and topiary plants. In the adjacent crab-apple allée, I staggered the trees to improve the view from the pool area. The allée extends to the end of the property, creating a vista that leads the eye to a lovely old birdhouse designed for purple martins. These birds feed mainly on mosquitoes so they make it easier to enjoy evenings in the garden.

The neighbors put in a tennis court on the north side that at times is very noisy. For screening we created two sets of plantings. First a row of arborvitae (*Thuja occidentalis* 'Nigra') was added along

Phlox, geraniums and herbs in clay pots are part of this perennial garden just off the terrace.

This crab-apple allée (Malus floribunda) *leads toward an unusual birdhouse for purple martins, which serves as the focal point.*

This small birch grove with bench and sundial makes a quiet retreat.

the property line. These evergreens help absorb sound. Second, a trellis garden was designed (list 3). Opposite the terrace, a tall lattice fence provides a sound barrier, and serves as an attractive accent around a small grove of birch trees. Here we planted ferns, myrtle with snowdrops, snowflakes, early spring bulbs, white wood hyacinths and white *Cleome*. A small bench and a sundial complete this quiet retreat. The two screens, one natural and one architectural, succeed in reducing the noise level from the tennis court and have the added advantage of making the garden more private.

The owners wanted a swimming pool and space for entertaining. A lap pool fits in behind the garage with spacious sitting areas beneath a grape arbor at the edge of the open lawn. A line of hydrangeas (*Hydrangea arborescens, H. macrophylla* 'Nikko Blue' and *H. macrophylla* 'Compacta') gives the pool a feeling of enclosure and produces masses of summer blooms, as does a fence covered with trumpet vines.

The latest addition is a much-used summer room with lovely views of the garden (list 4). Plantings of cotoneaster (*Cotoneaster horizontalis*), dwarf boxwood (*Buxus microphylla koreana*) and leucothoe (*Leucothoe Fontanesiana*) form a pleasant arrangement for the foundation of this addition. A new door was added to give direct access from the porch to the garden. A pine (*Pinus parviflora*) underplanted

This view of the lap pool adjacent to a sitting terrace behind the garage shows the grape arbor planted on the trellis with red impatiens below. A Rose of Sharon at the corner of the garage has lovely white blossoms for several weeks in late summer.

with spring bulbs and the groundcover myrtle (*Vinca minor*) makes this corner planting an easily maintained spot.

The area between the new addition and the garage (just 15 feet wide) is connected with a lattice fence, creating a warm, sunny spot for camellias. A lattice fence is also used to enclose the pool. In this part of Long Island, pools must be fenced in, but in order to avoid a closed-in feeling, the owners have placed the fence along the property line. To soften the fence and screen the neighbors, I added a border of hybrid rhododendron, Leyland cypress (× *Cupressocyparis Leylandii*) and multistemmed shadblow trees (*Amelanchier canadensis*). An old cherry tree was removed just behind the pool and was replaced by a European beech (*Fagus sylvatica*), which the owners had always wanted (list 5).

Every garden should include a work space, and here it is at the east side of the garage, where it provides plenty of room for storage space as well.

One of the things I love best about this little unpretentious house and grounds is the spacious feeling achieved by stretches of open lawn. The plan isn't complicated, but it is interesting—as one strolls the property, there is something different at every turn.

PLANT LIST

LIST 1 ❧ SCREEN PLANTING

Cornus Kousa Chinensis (Chinese dogwood)

Ilex opaca (American holly)

Juniperus virginiana (Cedar)

Picea glauca (Spruce)

Pinus Strobus (White pine)

Rhododendron maximum (Rosebay rhododendron)

Viburnum rhytidophyllum (Leather-leaf viburnum)

Viburnum tomentosum (Double file viburnum)

LIST 2 ❧ FLOWER BORDER (OLD-FASHIONED FLOWERS)

Achillea Hybrid 'Moonshine' (Yarrow)

Althaea rosea (Hibiscus)

Aquilegia canadensis (Columbine)

Asclepias tuberosa (Butterfly weed)

Aster ×*Frikartii* (Aster)

Astilbe ×*Arendsii* 'Deutschland' (Astilbe)

Dianthus 'Her Majesty' (Carnation)

Echinops exaltatus (Globe thistle)

Geranium Endressii (Cranesbill)

Iris, in variety (Iris)

Lupinus polyphyllus (Lupine)

Nepeta Mussinii (Catmint)

Papaver orientale (Oriental poppy)

Phlox carolina 'Miss Lingard' (Phlox)

Salvia officinalis (Garden sage)

Veronica longifolia subsessilis (Speedwell)

LIST 3 ❧ TRELLIS GARDEN

Adiantum pedatum (Maidenhair fern)

Betula alba (White Birch)

Impatiens (Impatiens)

Polypodium virginianum (Common polypody)

Scilla sibirica (Squill)

Thelypteris noveboracensis (New York fern)

LIST 4 ❧ PLANTING AROUND SUMMER ROOM

Abelia grandiflora 'Sherwoodi' (Abelia)

Buxus sempervirens 'Vardar Valley' (Boxwood)

Callicarpa japonica (Japanese beautyberry)

Corylopsis spicata (Winter hazel)

Cotoneaster horizontalis (Cotoneaster)

Daphne ×*Burkwoodii* 'Carol Mackie' (Daphne)

Ilex pedunculosa (Longstalk holly)

Jasminum nudiflorum (Jasmine)

Lagerstroemia ×*amabilis* (Crape myrtle)

Leucothoe Fontanesiana (Drooping leucothoe)

Rhododendron 'Joseph Hill' (Azalea)

Rhododendron 'Sir Robert' (Azalea)

Rhododendron 'Wintergreen' (Azalea)

LIST 5 ❧ BACK BOUNDARY PLANTING

Acer rubrum (Red maple)

Amelanchier canadensis (Shadblow tree)

×*Cupressocyparis Leylandii* (Leyland cypress)

Fagus sylvatica (Beech tree)

Ilex ×*Meserveae* 'Blue Princess' (Blue holly)

Ilex opaca (American holly)

Oxydendrum arboreum (Sourwood)

Rhododendron catawbiense 'Album' (Rhododendron)

Rhododendron 'Scintillation' (Rhododendron)

Rhododendron 'Weston' (Rhododendron)

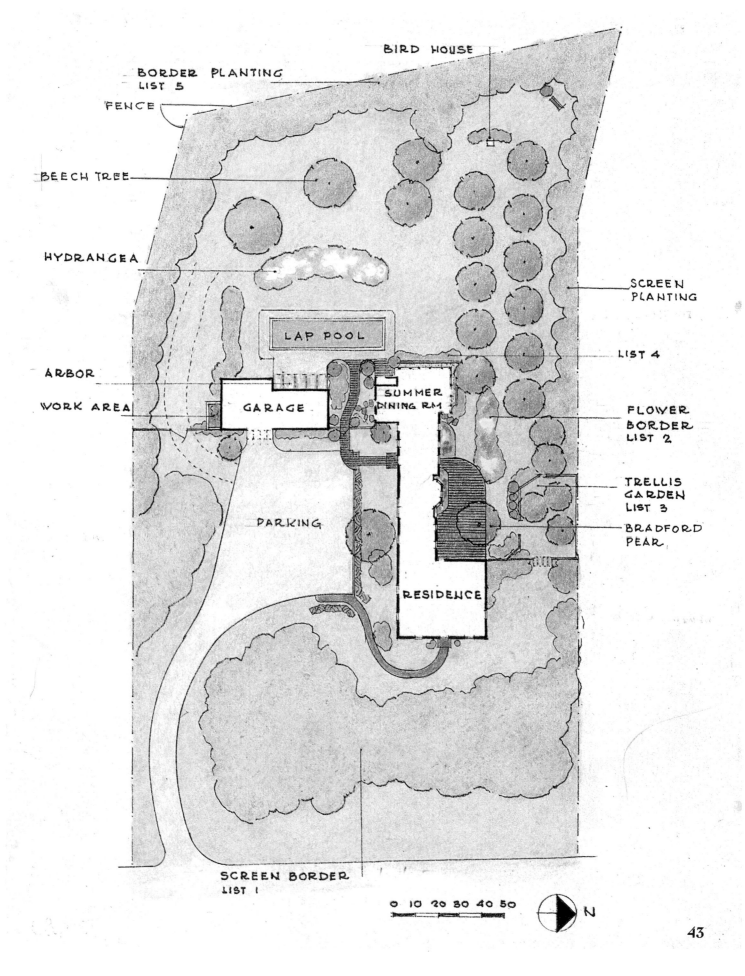

BIRD HOUSE

BORDER PLANTING
LIST 5

FENCE

BEECH TREE

HYDRANGEA

SCREEN
PLANTING

LAP POOL

LIST 4

ARBOR

WORK AREA

GARAGE

SUMMER
DINING RM

FLOWER
BORDER
LIST 2

TRELLIS
GARDEN
LIST 3

BRADFORD
PEAR

PARKING

RESIDENCE

SCREEN BORDER
LIST 1

0 10 20 30 40 50

N

CHAPTER 6

A Contemporary Home with a Waterfall

The redesign of a 24 × 32–foot flagstone terrace set between the wings of a contemporary house on one acre and shaded by a Norway maple (*Acer platanoides*) was the focus of our work in this garden. The maple was the only plant that had survived a disastrous fire in which the family had lost their previous home and everything in it. The new house was built in a few months around this old tree. It was very different from their lovely old home, but for a couple with three sons, building quickly was necessary. Now, gazing at the new house's flagstone terrace, we wondered how the terrace could be improved to take advantage of the site.

I suggested a little waterfall connecting three sitting areas (list 1). The design that evolved included a stream that came up out of the pavement in one corner of a deck and meandered some 15 feet to a small pool 4 feet below. The owners had recently taken a trip to Japan and returned with a handsome lantern, and the side of this pool turned out to be an ideal place to display it. A large stepping-stone leads from this upper deck to the next level. The lower flagstone terrace has a sitting wall of railroad ties with a wide plank as the coping. Descending another few steps, to the grass area, you reach another terrace, added for large groups. Flagstone laid in an irregular pattern is set with wide grass joints. This lower terrace looks out on a swimming pool and small rose garden adjacent to it (list 2). Junipers and summer flowers outline the edge of the pool—

A tiny stream flows between the deck and the terrace. Holly (Ilex convexa) has been planted here, along with Korean boxwoods and pachysandra as a groundcover. The Korean boxwood is repeated beneath the Norway maple and one Japanese maple provides a background for the Japanese lantern.

An old Norway maple shades this terrace set between the wings of a contemporary house.

some years it is all in gray foliage, other years in color. The rose garden has five varieties of roses that were selected for their color, and planted four feet apart to allow room to develop. Below this rose garden is an open area for vegetables. It is well below the pool so one can overlook it to the view beyond.

The deck and terraces were the first part of the planning, but I also redesigned the entrance to the house and replanted along the property lines with shadblow (*Amelanchier canadensis*), Chinese dogwood (*Cornus Kousa Chinensis*), azaleas (*Rhododendron mucronatum* 'Delaware Valley White') and rhododendron (*R.* 'Scintillation') (list 3). The front door was partially hidden by these plants, so to make a more interesting approach a flagstone terrace was added with a wide path from the parking area. The plants used near the house were rhododendron (*R.* Hybrid 'Boule de Neige'), leucothoe (*Leucothoe Fontanesiana*) and some glossy Japanese hollies (*Ilex crenata*) by the door. A climbing hydrangea (*Hydrangea petiolaris*) clings to the stone chimney and has developed into a beautiful vine with lovely white flowers in June.

A few years later, the owners decided to add a whole complex for their children and grandchildren. This included a children's terrace and play space and a wonderful deck that can be used by young and old. There is a circular stair from the upper deck down to

The stream starts at the corner of the house and meanders through the rocks to the lower terrace. Japanese andromeda *and Korean boxwoods complete the plantings in this corner.*

the play area where the grandchildren have plenty of space for games. The entrance to this wing is marked by a pair of birch trees (*Betula pendula* 'Gracilis') and hollies (*Ilex × Meserveae*) with an edging of Korean boxwood (*Buxus microphylla koreana*) and a groundcover of myrtle (*Vinca minor*).

Neighbors can sometimes pose problems; here it was necessary to screen a large new house and fence out the owner's bull terriers (list 4). This was accomplished with a tall chain link fence screened by a planting of hemlocks (*Tsuga canadensis*), pines (*Pinus Strobus*) and flowering shrubs—forsythia (*Forsythia × intermedia*), mock orange (*Philadelphus coronarius*), buddleia (*Buddleia Davidii*) and Rose of Sharon (*Hibiscus syriacus*)—all selected for their continuous bloom. This made a dense planting that effectively hides the house and dog pens.

What has made this plan remarkable is the fact that with few flowers, this really is a delightful green garden visible from every room in the house. It is especially pleasant in the summer when you can step out of the living room onto a deck that overlooks the garden. The sound of water falling over the rocks is refreshing, and the plants—Japanese andromeda (*Pieris japonica*), leucothoe (*L. Fontanesiana*), common bamboo (*Bambusa vulgaris*) and Korean boxwood (*Buxus microphylla koreana*)—are always in scale for this little place.

It is wise to note that bamboo can become invasive, so here it is planted in metal tubs. Some cold winters it dies back, but we prune it heavily and new shoots will start in early spring to give the lovely airy feeling this plant imparts and the privacy needed for the bedroom windows.

From the end of these terraces is the bonus of a spectacular view of the distant Manhattan skyline—a wonderful mix of being near the city while still in the country.

Left: Near the children's terrace a weeping birch, 'The Fairy' rose and rock cotoneaster are planted over a low wall.

PLANT LIST

LIST 1 ❧ TERRACE PLANTING

Bambusa vulgaris (Common bamboo)

Buxus microphylla koreana (Korean boxwood)

Cotoneaster horizontalis (Cotoneaster)

Pieris japonica (Japanese andromeda)

Vinca minor (Periwinkle, myrtle)

LIST 2 ❧ POOL PLANTING

Juniperus communis 'Hornibrookii' (Juniper)

Juniperus horizontalis 'Wiltonii' (Juniper)

Juniperus Sargentii (Juniper)

Rosa 'Americana' (Rose)

Rosa floribunda 'Betty Prior' (Rose)

Rosa 'Peace' (Rose)

Rosa polyantha 'The Fairy' (Rose)

Rosa 'Queen Elizabeth' (Rose)

Gray Flowers

Achillea Hybrid 'Moonshine' (Yarrow)

Artemisia Stellerana (Hardy dusty miller)

Phalaris arundinacea picta (Ribbon grass)

LIST 3 ❧ ENTRANCE PLANTING

Amelanchier canadensis (Downy shadblow)

Cornus Kousa Chinensis (Chinese dogwood)

Ilex crenata 'Bullata' (Box-leaved holly)

Ilex crenata (Japanese holly)

Rhododendron maximum (Rosebay rhododendron)

Rhododendron mucronatum 'Delaware Valley White' (Azalea)

Rhododendron 'Scintillation' (Rhododendron)

LIST 4 ❧ SCREEN PLANTING

Buddleia Davidii (Butterfly bush)

Euonymus alata (Burning bush)

Forsythia × intermedia (Forsythia)

Hibiscus syriacus (Rose of Sharon)

Philadelphus coronarius (Mock orange)

Picea Omorika (Serbian spruce)

Pinus Strobus (White pine)

Tsuga canadensis (Hemlock)

Viburnum tomentosum (Double file viburnum)

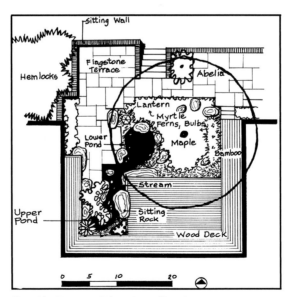

Detail: Terrace Planting (list 1).

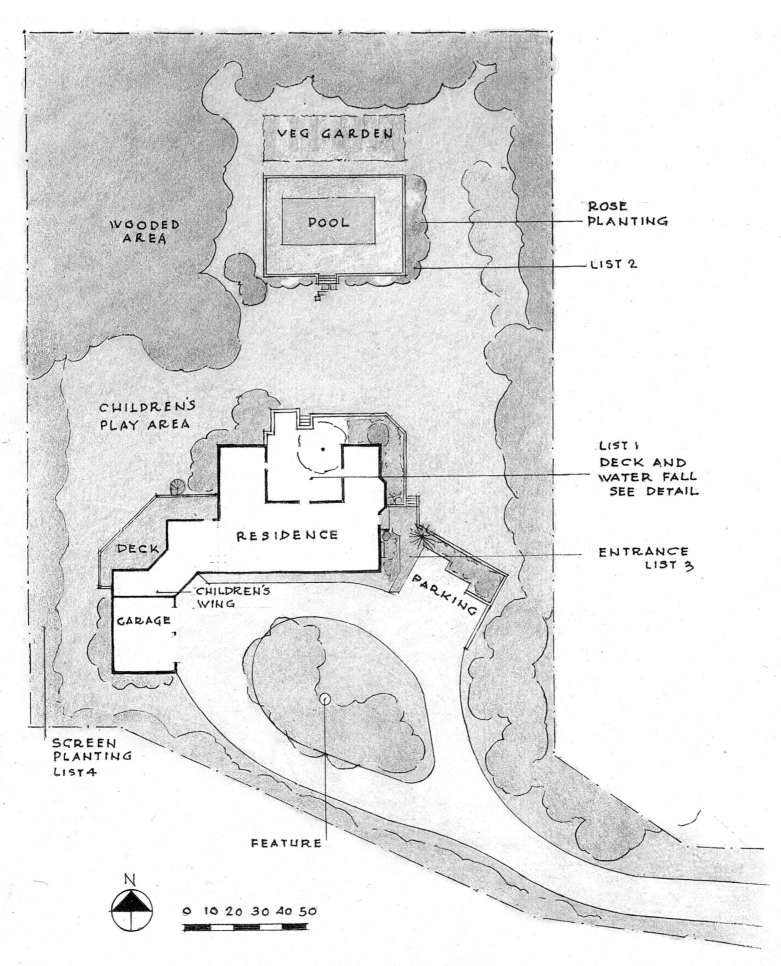

VEG GARDEN

WOODED AREA

POOL

ROSE PLANTING

LIST 2

CHILDREN'S PLAY AREA

LIST 1
DECK AND
WATER FALL
SEE DETAIL

RESIDENCE

DECK

CHILDREN'S WING

GARAGE

ENTRANCE
LIST 3

PARKING

SCREEN PLANTING LIST 4

FEATURE

N

0 10 20 30 40 50

PART III

Three to Five Acres

There are several kinds of iris along the water and several varieties of hostas and astilbe, which give summer bloom, looking down over the waterfall to the pool and the meadow beyond.

CHAPTER 7

Many Garden Rooms

A garden can be designed with different rooms, just as there are different rooms in a house. Each room has its own special feeling, purpose and color scheme. This property of 3½ acres features many garden rooms. Each room has its special feeling and special flowers, and each has been enjoyed at dawn, at sunset and on rainy days under umbrellas. The owners use the garden as a place for restoration and refreshment.

I think back to the first conversations I had with the owners and the things they wanted: a boxwood walk reminiscent of those in Virginia's colonial gardens, an allée for spring-flowering trees with masses of peonies and summer annuals, a small perennial garden, a gazebo from which to enjoy summer flowers and a collection of rhododendron and azaleas. Eventually, near a guest cottage there would be a swimming pool and a croquet court.

Passing from the house out through a wide door onto a brick terrace, one sees a panoramic view of the gardens. This large, curved brick terrace was planned for dinner parties of 18 and has a brick sitting wall. It is shaded by the branches of a weeping willow, and it is a delightful spot from which to admire the three formal elements arranged in an informal plan.

The central element is a boxwood walk, gently curved to draw the eye to the end of the property. Slightly to the left, a pair of crab apples frame a view to a gazebo that overlooks a circular garden

The boxwood walk leading to the guesthouse is seen through the branches of an old cedar tree. These boxwoods, although recently planted, look as though they have been in place for many years.

The gazebo at the end of the circular garden is flanked by two old trimmed yews with topiary cedar in front. The circular garden is filled with pink and pale yellow snapdragons and bronze-leaf begonias.

room with flowers and flowering shrubs. On the other side of the boxwood walk, a crab-apple allée leads from the window of a favorite sitting room to a small perennial garden planted in the shade of an old silver bell tree (*Halesia carolina*). These features blend well together because they are surrounded by a generous expanse of open lawn and a stand of towering trees. The informal feeling is strengthened by plantings of flowering shrubs that provide color throughout the summer.

The garden's central path is the long, curving boxwood walk. Two urns filled with annuals accent the entrance; beyond them, the 30 large specimen boxwoods (*Buxus microphylla* 'Suffruticosa'), each 4 × 5 feet, were planted to lead toward the future guesthouse and swimming pool. The walk is very visible from the house—most notably from a large window in the main stairway. This view looks through two old trees, a willow (*Salix pentandra*) with arching branches that comes to the ground and a beautiful old plume cypress (*Chamaecyparis pisifera* 'Plumosa'), which is another ancient variety of tree with lovely lines.'

Another important terrace view includes a pair of Japanese flowering crab apples (*Malus floribunda*) framing the entrance to the circular garden (list 1). The gazebo draws you toward the far side of this garden room. From the gazebo is a lovely view of the round

Right: *A crab-apple allée is planted with ribbons of pink and white impatiens for a splashy summer effect. The yew hedge at the end has a small lead statue, with more pink impatiens below.*

garden's banked beds. In summer they are filled with hundreds of pink and pale yellow snapdragons, blue heliotropes, blue salvias, yellow coreopsis, blue ageratums and ribbons of bronze-leaf begonias. Beyond the masses of bloom are mature hillus, viburnums, yews, spireas and butterfly bushes. Eventually, an oval rhododendron garden will be planted beyond the gazebo. It will lead back toward the guesthouse and swimming pool.

To the right of the boxwood walk is the crab-apple allée (*Malus* 'Snowdrift'), underplanted with peonies and tulips in spring (list 2). Later, masses of impatiens are planted in a ribbonlike design of light to dark pinks for continuous summer bloom. The crab apples hold their lovely orange fruit well into the winter. In the evening, when covered with thousands of droplets of dew and illuminated by soft underlighting, they provide a fairyland picture. Tall arborvitae (*Thuja occidentalis* 'Pyramidalis') have been planted as a background for the allée, and as a screen for the garage. A mixture of flowering shrubs—crape myrtles, vitexes, hydrangeas and caryopteris—grows in front of the hedge. This planting is basically blue, and effective in part because the adjacent impatiens add a splash of warmer color.

At the end of the allée a little perennial garden room is enclosed with a yew hedge (*Taxus* ×*media* 'Hicksii'). An old silver bell tree (*Halesia carolina*) produces a lot of shade, so I had to select an unusual combination of plants (list 3). A *Magnolia grandiflora* grows just outside of the hedge, producing lovely, fragrant summer flowers and stunning red fruit. This southern tree must be protected from winter winds.

As the owner says, "Who knows what will be next? A garden is never really finished. Every flower and tree can be another happy adventure. My husband and I dreamed our dreams, reminisced and planned for many years in our ever-changing garden. It is still changing in much the way we had planned before he died. I can still sit in each of the garden rooms and dream of yesterdays, and it is a good feeling. Precious times are never lost, especially when shared in a garden."

In the corner of the perennial garden, a circular bench surrounds an old silver bell tree (Halesia). *From here one sees the small perennial garden enclosed with the yew hedge. Clumps of* Astilbe × Arendsii *'Deutschland' and impatiens grow well in the shade.*

PLANT LIST

LIST 1 ❧ CIRCULAR GARDEN
SHRUB PLANTING

Abelia ×*grandiflora* (Abelia)

Buddleia Davidii 'Empire Blue'

Ilex ×*Meserveae* 'Blue Princess' (Blue holly)

Ilex pedunculosa (Longstalk holly)

Malus floribunda (Flowering crab apple)

Picea 'Nidiformis' (Nest spruce)

Spiraea nipponica 'Snowmound' (Spirea)

Spiraea 'Primrose' (Spirea)

Taxus cuspidata (Yew)

Thuja occidentalis 'Nigra' (Dark American arborvitae)

Viburnum tomentosum (Double file viburnum)

Annuals fill a four-foot bed and change from year to year

LIST 2 ❧ CRAB-APPLE ALLÉE

Caryopteris 'Blue Mist' (Blue spirea)

Hydrangea macrophylla 'Nikko Blue' (Hydrangea)

Hydrangea paniculata 'Grandiflora' (Peegee hydrangea)

Impatiens, in variety (Impatiens)

Lagerstroemia ×*amabilis* 'Natchez' (Crape myrtle; white)

Lagerstroemia ×*amabilis* 'Potomac' (Crape myrtle; pink)

Magnolia virginiana glauca (Sweet bay)

Paeonia 'Angelus' (pink)

Paeonia 'Elsa Sass' (white)

Paeonia lactiflora 'Festiva maxima' (white)

Paeonia 'Le Cygne' (white)

Paeonia 'Monsieur Jules Elie' (pink)

Paeonia 'Myrtle Gentry' (pink)

Paeonia 'Pink Parfait' (pink)

Paeonia 'Raspberry Sundae' (pink)

Paeonia suffruticosa 'Godaishu' (Tree peony)

Vitex Agnus-castus 'Latifolia' (Chaste tree)

LIST 3 ❧ SMALL SHADY
PERENNIAL GARDEN

Aconitum Napellus (Monkshood)

Anemone japonica 'Mont Rose' (Anemone)

Aquilegia caerulea (Columbine)

Aster ×*Frikartii* (Aster or Michaelmas daisy)

Astilbe 'Bridal Veil' (Astilbe)

Astilbe chinensis 'Pumila' (Astilbe)

Astilbe 'Gladstone' (Astilbe)

Astilbe ×*rosea* 'Peach Blossom' (Astilbe)

Astilbe simplicifolia 'Sprite' (Astilbe)

Astilbe Thunbergii 'Professor Van der Weilen' (Astilbe)

Brunnera macrophylla or *Anchusa myosotidiflora* (Bugloss)

Dicentra spectabilis 'Alba' (Bleeding heart)

Geranium Endressii 'Johnson's Blue' (Cranesbill)

Iberis sempervirens 'Purity' (Candytuft)

Iris 'Full Tide' (Bearded iris)

Iris 'Modern Classic' (Bearded iris)

Iris sibirica 'Lady Godiva' (Siberian iris)

Iris sibirica 'Mountain Lake' (Siberian iris)

Lavandula angustifolia 'Hidcote' (Lavender)

Lilium regale (Regal lily)

Lilium rubrum (Rubrum lily)

Lupinus 'Russell' Hybrids (Lupine)

Paeonia lactiflora 'Festiva Maxima' (Peony)

Phlox paniculata 'Fairest One' (Phlox)

Platycodon grandiflorus 'Mariesii' (Balloon flower; blue)

Veronica spicata 'Blue Charm' (Speedwell)

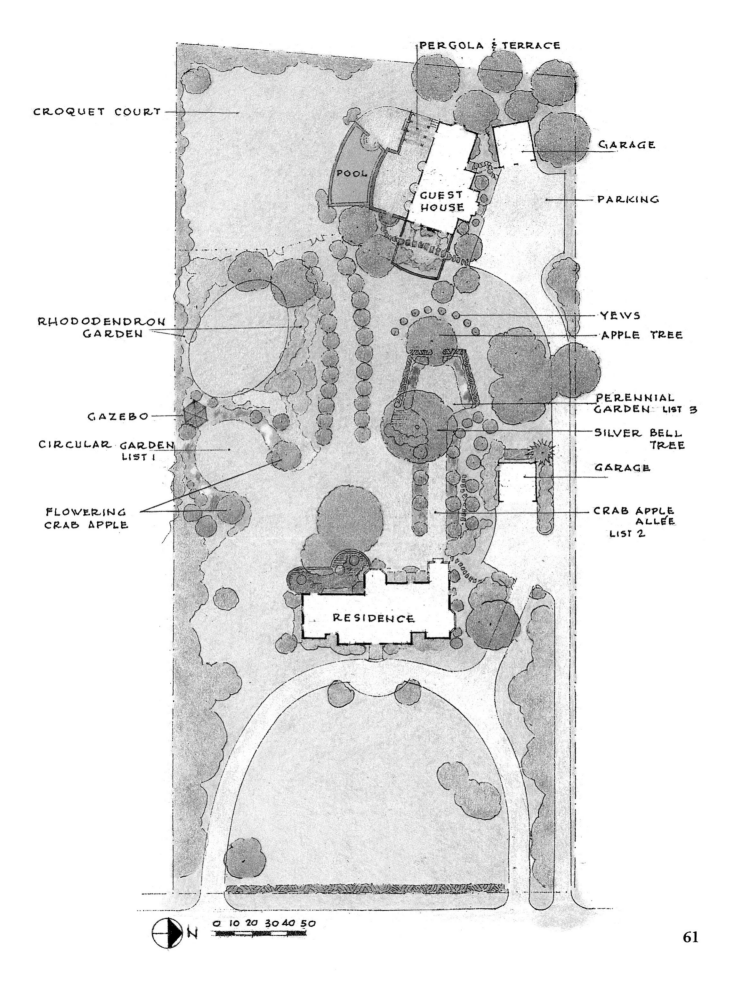

CROQUET COURT

PERGOLA & TERRACE

GARAGE

POOL

GUEST HOUSE

PARKING

RHODODENDRON GARDEN

YEWS

APPLE TREE

PERENNIAL GARDEN LIST 3

GAZEBO

SILVER BELL TREE

CIRCULAR GARDEN LIST 1

GARAGE

FLOWERING CRAB APPLE

CRAB APPLE ALLEE LIST 2

RESIDENCE

0 10 20 30 40 50

N

CHAPTER 8

A Hillside Planting with Waterfall

A dramatic change in grade makes planning a garden a challenge. Grading involves moving soil (both topsoil and subsoil) to create a level area around a house or play space (pool or tennis court), or perennial garden to create a proper area that is easy to walk on or drive on. Grading is also used to solve problems such as wet spots, slopes to prevent erosion and other troublesome areas on your property. Grading is the most important part of a landscape development and, therefore, should be done correctly because it is very expensive to redo.

On a 3½-acre property this house is situated on a hill overlooking a busy road. The driveway was widened to allow adequate parking, and steps to the front door were planted with rhododendron, hydrangeas and a groundcover of ivy. A 20-foot drop on the garden side separates the main house from a large meadow, gazebo, children's play area, vegetable garden and swimming pool. It was imperative to get up and down this steep slope in an easy, safe way. A railroad-tie ramp with grass treads had not proved successful.

I met the owners in the summer of 1984 and suggested that we enlarge the sitting terrace and construct a waterfall down this steep grade. This waterfall and a series of curving wooden steps proved to be a good solution to a very difficult problem.

To provide views of the pool and lower garden, I built a large brick terrace with a pierced brick sitting wall. This wall with its regular openings gives glimpses of the plantings below (list 1). The start of the waterfall is just below the terrace near a swamp red

A simple wooden bridge crosses the stream where water hyacinths grow. Siberian iris and astilbe grow along the edges.

The steep bank off the house and terrace is planted with daylilies, a few specimen evergreens and iris.

maple (*Acer rubrum*). This tree gives shade to the terrace on hot summer days, and has a brilliant fall color. Here I planted plants that tolerate water well: ferns, Japanese iris, ivy, lobelia and marsh marigolds (list 2).

Alongside the waterfall, a winding flight of steps leads down the bank in much the same way that the water flows, with wide steps where the water moves slowly and steeper steps where the stream drops quickly over rocks. A flat ramp leads to a little bridge over the brook. Here one can stop to see a small natural pond with water lilies and carp, where white *Buddleia* bushes are magnets for butterflies in summer and the sound of water is everywhere. (Note: The flow of water can easily be adjusted.)

Safety was a consideration, so I felt it was important to design a railing for these steps. A simple pipe railing proved the best choice. It was camouflaged by a planting of fleece vine (*Polygonum Aubertii*). Although this vine can grow as much as 40 feet during a season, it can easily be controlled by frequent pruning. It produces masses of tiny white flowers in late August.

The overall planting for this steep slope included two flowering trees close to the terrace, on the right a styrax (*Styrax japonicus*), and on the left, a fall-blooming cherry (*Prunus autumnalis*). Between the trees, a holly hedge (*Ilex ×Meserveae* 'Blue Princess') circles the wall, giving it an evergreen frame that makes it look less imposing. Plantings on the bank include hundreds of daylilies that bloom from June to September (list 3).

A Japanese lantern accents the approach to the bridge. Astilbe *and* Hypericum *are planted on the banks here.*

At the bottom of the bank, a garden adjacent to the pool terrace and visible from the upper terrace is filled with summer-blooming annuals. When I began the landscaping I used only low flowers so the children's playhouse and surrounding area could be seen. That has now changed; because the children are older, visibility is no longer critical. Clumps of tall phlox, asters and larkspurs have been added. But the playhouse is still often used and is a charming sight when the fleece vine covers it.

The meadow was cut back to provide more play space. Wildflowers and a cut-leaf beech (*Fagus sylvatica*) have been added to give color, and now this is a lovely area to look down on.

The gazebo near the pool was designed to be a shady sitting place for those who like to be out of the sun. The fast-growing fleece vine has completely covered it. This gazebo overlooks an orchard and vegetable garden, which provides this family of vegetarians with food throughout the summer. One can even see a little wooden building that houses the sauna tucked into the hillside. On that slope, winding stone steps will climb the hill toward the rhododendron garden. This garden (list 4) was developed when an addition to the house was built. Rhododendron, azaleas and summer annuals provide color around a flagpole. (This was especially requested by the owner, who enjoys raising the flag when he's in residence.)

The terrace, lower pool area and play space are all constantly in use either for family activities or large gatherings. Thus the

The gazebo, covered with fleece vine, is a delightful place to sit out of the sun near the swimming pool. Daylilies bloom throughout the summer.

A fenced vegetable garden produces enough vegetables for this family of four.

construction of the waterfall and wooden steps have tied the two areas together in a way that has proved both convenient and interesting.

PLANT LIST

LIST 1 ✎ HILLSIDE GARDEN

Buddleia Davidii 'Pink Delight' (Butterfly bush)

Caryopteris ✕ *clandonesis* 'Blue Mist' (Blue spirea)

Hypericum calycinum 'Hidcote' (St - John's-wort)

Iris ensata 'Moonlight Waves' (Japanese iris)

Iris ensata 'Ruby King' (Japanese iris)

Picea Abies 'Clanbrasiliana' (Dwarf spruce)

Potentilla fruticosa 'Primrose Beauty' (Cinquefoil)

LIST 2 ✎ PLANTINGS ALONG WATERFALL

Adiantum pedatum (Maidenhair fern)

Caltha palustris (Marsh marigolds)

Hedera Helix 'Baltica' (Baltic ivy)

Iris Kaempferi (Japanese iris)

Lobelia siphilitica (Lobelia)

Osmunda cinnamomea (Cinnamon fern)

LIST 3 ✎ DAYLILY PLANTING (*Hemerocallis*)

'Canary Glow'

'Eenie Weenie'

'Flava'

'Hyperion'

'Lemona'

'Lemon Drops'

'Mrs. Wyman'

'Prairie Moonlight'

'Star Dreams'

'Stella d'Oro'

'Suzy Wong'

LIST 4 ✎ RHODODENDRON GARDEN

Rhododendron arborescens (Azalea)

Rhododendron catawbiense 'Roseum Elegans' (Rhododendron)

Rhododendron Hybrid 'Boule de Neige' (Rhododendron)

Rhododendron Hybrid 'Chionoides' (Rhododendron)

Rhododendron Hybrid 'Waltham' (Rhododendron)

Rhododendron Schlippenbachii (Azalea)

Rhododendron Vaseyi (Azalea)

Rhododendron viscosum (Azalea)

Summer Annuals (change each year)

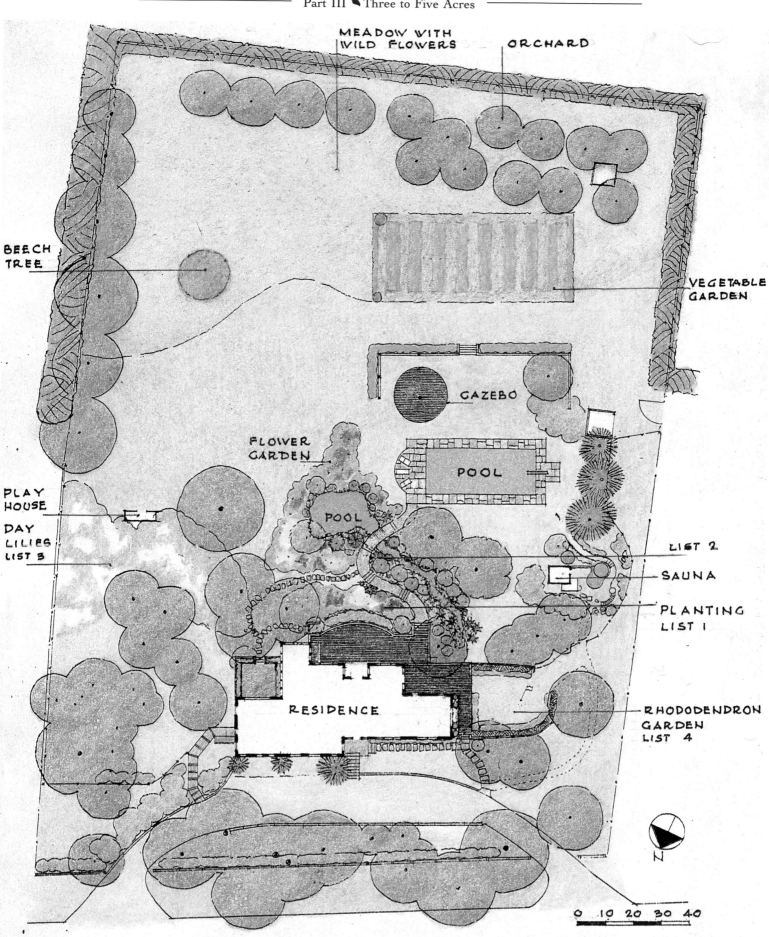

MEADOW WITH
WILD FLOWERS

ORCHARD

BEECH
TREE

VEGETABLE
GARDEN

GAZEBO

FLOWER
GARDEN

POOL

PLAY
HOUSE

POOL

LIST 2

DAY
LILIES
LIST 3

SAUNA

PLANTING
LIST 1

RESIDENCE

RHODODENDRON
GARDEN
LIST 4

N

0   10   20   30   40

67

CHAPTER 9

A Tranquil Setting

This colonial home is on a 3-acre site along a village street on Long Island. At the back of the house, sitting on the covered porch adjacent to a large terrace, one feels total serenity—exactly what a very busy couple wanted on their weekend visits.

The rolling grounds were planted in the early 1900s with a variety of evergreens, cypress, arborvitae, spruce, pine and yew—all of these have grown extremely well in a seaside environment just 500 feet from the ocean. There are also existing oaks, maples, birches and a wonderful old silk tree (*Albizia Julibrissin*). This tree doesn't leaf-out until June, but then develops very quickly and is a beautiful summer-flowering specimen. The property had a lovely, parklike feeling that the clients appreciated and wanted to preserve and enhance.

To supplement the existing planting, I have added plane trees (*Platanus acerifolia*) along the drive, red maples (*Acer rubrum*) in the lawn and hollies (*Ilex opaca*) to hide a nearby building across the street. Chinese dogwood (*Cornus Kousa Chinensis*), tree lilacs (*Syringa japonica*), a magnolia (*Magnolia stellata*) and a Japanese maple (*Acer palmatum*) have also been added. More recently a Japanese cedar (*Cryptomeria japonica* 'Lobbii'), sourwood (*Oxydendrum arboreum*) and dawn redwood (*Metasequoia glyptostroboides*) were planted in one of the borders. A fern-leaf beech (*Fagus sylvatica* 'Asplenifolia') opposite the

A stepping-stone path through the Ajuga leads to a lovely old birdhouse set among the lilacs.

A dry stream meanders along the edge of the property. Iris, coral-bells and Leucothoe *have been chosen because they are interesting plants to use in a limited space.*

dining room window has lovely lacey form, and is beautiful in fall with brilliant yellow color.

Lining the street, old plane trees and a tall privet hedge help give the needed protection from the salt spray and winds. The informal driveway (list 1) with its circular turnaround leads to the front door, where white azaleas (*Azalea Daviesii*), boxwood (*Buxus sempervirens*) and longstalk holly (*Ilex pedunculosa*) flank each side of the steps. Containers on the front porch are filled with pink geraniums, which are repeated in the window box on the second floor. A clump of Hinoki cypress in the curve of the driveway gives protection to this entrance.

Accepting existing conditions is often necessary, be they good or bad: Here, a long, straight concrete walk had been used by neighbors for access to a nearby lake. We felt it was necessary to leave this walk, but by adding some topsoil, and allowing grass to grow over one section, we managed to create a more desirable, natural-looking path. Next we built a dry stream that curves along the path to a shady area where violets, *Ajuga, Iris cristata*, hostas and some flowering shrubs have been planted (list 2). A dry stream is a shallow area that does not hold water, but gives the illusion of doing so. We used a dry stream instead of a real stream as it is more economical to build and easier to maintain. You start by digging a trough varying in depth from 6 to 18 inches. This is lined with polyethylene and covered with stones 2 to 5 inches in size.

About a third of the way down the walk it becomes even more shady, because the old trees have grown together. Ferns, lilies of the valley, ivy and hostas were planted here. Continuing still farther, the dry stream leads to a small, hidden terrace with a little pool and waterfall (list 3). Here a holly hedge (*I. latifolia*) was planted to screen the fencing. *Mazus reptans*, a quick-spreading prostrate groundcover, grows between the stepping-stones and *Vinca minor* at the edge of the pool. Several *Iris sibirica* give a spot of color in early June, followed by little, low *Astilbe chinensis* 'Pumila' in midsummer. This is a quiet place to read and have tea.

The remaining path is given over to lilacs, with drifts of daffodils planted below. This section is a joy to see in April and again in May when the lilacs (*Syringa vulgaris* 'Ellen Willmott', *S. Meyeri* 'Palabin', *S.* ×*prestoniae* 'James McFarlane' and *S.* 'Perseca') bloom. Two beautiful lead deer add a most charming touch. Below the lilacs, bugleweed (*Ajuga reptans* 'Purpurea') with its purple blossoms covers the ground and blooms for several weeks.

Mazus, a good creeping groundcover, softens the edges of a small pool beside a terrace. Myrtle has been planted behind the pool, and one water lily and two water hyacinths have been placed in the pool.

Astilbe grows en masse along the edge of the flowering shrub border. Ligularia is just starting to bloom.

Near the end of the walk, a toolhouse is hidden among the hemlocks. What is noticeable is a tree wisteria, equally attractive in winter or summer. Also nearby is a wide, mixed border that extends along the length of the property line (list 4). This border, visible from the terrace, is planted with drifts of geraniums, forget-me-nots, astilbe, asters and snow-on-the-mountain. It is backed with flowering shrubs and some hemlocks.

The large brick terrace off of the living room and library has a sitting wall with a broad step down to the lawn. Borders of spring-blooming tulips, summer-blooming perennials and *Rosa polyantha* 'The Fairy' rose flank this opening (list 5). It is lovely to look at from the terrace, and makes a nice frame of color throughout the summer. Pots of impatiens and shasta daisies are also used on the terrace. On the north side of the terrace, a narrow, shady bed contains two espaliered pear trees. Skimmias and daphnes planted between the espaliers provide green color in winter. A weeping birch (*Betula pendula* 'Youngii') ends this little planting bed.

This terrace is protected by an awning, and it has become the most-used spot on the property. From here, looking out on the open lawn, one feels the quietness and serenity that were my clients' primary objectives.

This narrow perennial border has tulips for cutting in the spring followed by astilbe, iris, phlox, delphinium and Shasta daisies for summer bloom.

The bare branches of this wisteria in winter make a striking contrast to its grapelike clusters of flowers in summer.

PLANT LIST

LIST 1 ❧ DRIVEWAY ENTRANCE

Chamaecyparis obtusa (Cypress)

Euonymus radicans (Wintercreeper)

Ilex opaca (American holly)

Rhododendron 'Scintillation' (Rhododendron)

Taxus baccata 'Repandens' (Spreading English yew)

LIST 2 ❧ DRY STREAM
Shrubs

Hydrangea paniculata 'Grandiflora' (Peegee hydrangea)

Hypericum calycinum 'Hidcote' (St.-John's-wort)

Ilex glabra (Inkberry)

Ilex verticillata (Winterberry)

Rhododendron Schlippenbachii (Azalea)

Rhododendron Vaseyi (Azalea)

Rhododendron viscosum (Azalea)

Flowers

Ajuga reptans 'Purpurea' (Bugleweed)

Hosta, selected varities (Plantain lily)

Iris cristata (Iris)

Viola cornuta 'Jersey Gem' (Violet)

LIST 3 ❧ HIDDEN TERRACE WITH POOL

Astilbe chinensis 'Pumila' (Astilbe)

Draba sibirica (Draba)

Mazus reptans 'Album' (Mazus)

Rubus calucinoides 'Emerald Carpet' (Bramble)

Tradescantia ×Andersoniana (virginiana) (Virginia spiderwort)

Vinca minor 'Sterling Silver' (Periwinkle)

LIST 4 ❧ MIXED BORDER ALONG PROPERTY LINE
Shrubs

Cladrastis lutea (Yellowwood)

Cotinus Coggygria (Smoke bush)

Deutzia gracilis (Deutzia)

Hydrangea macrophylla 'Nikko Blue' (Hydrangea; blue)

Hydrangea paniculata 'Grandiflora' (Peegee hydrangea)

Ilex verticillata (Winterberry)

Metasequoia glyptostroboides (Dawn redwood)

Spiraea prunifolia (Spirea, bridal-wreath)

Spiraea nipponica 'Snowmound' (Spirea, bridal-wreath)

Weigela rosea (Weigela)

Wildflowers

Asclepias tuberosa (Butterfly weed)

Astilbe brautschleier (Astilbe)

Eupatorium coelestinum (Hardy ageratum, mist flower)

Euphorbia marginata (Snow-on-the-mountain)

Geranium Endressii 'Johnson's Blue' (Cranesbill)

Geranium sanguineum (Cranesbill)

Lamium album (White dead nettle)

Ligularia stenocephala 'The Rocket' (Ligularia)

Lobelia siphilitica (Blue cardinal flower)

Myosotis (Forget-me-not)

Salvia ×superba (Sage)

Thalictrum Rocheburnianum (Meadow rue)

LIST 5 ❧ TERRACE PLANTING

Anemone hupehensis japonica 'September Charm' (Windflower)

Aquilegia Hybrid 'Dragonfly' (Columbine)

Artemisia Schmidtiana 'Silver Mound' (Sagebrush, wormwood)

Aster ×Frikartii (Aster, Michaelmas daisy)

Astilbe Hybrid 'Bridal Veil' (Astilbe)

Dianthus 'Her Majesty' (Carnation)

Lilium auratum (Lily; white)

Lupinus 'Russell' Hybrids (Lupine; blue)

Salvia grandiflora (Sage)

Sedum spectabile 'Autumn Joy' (Stonecrop)

Veronica spicata 'Icicle' (Speedwell)

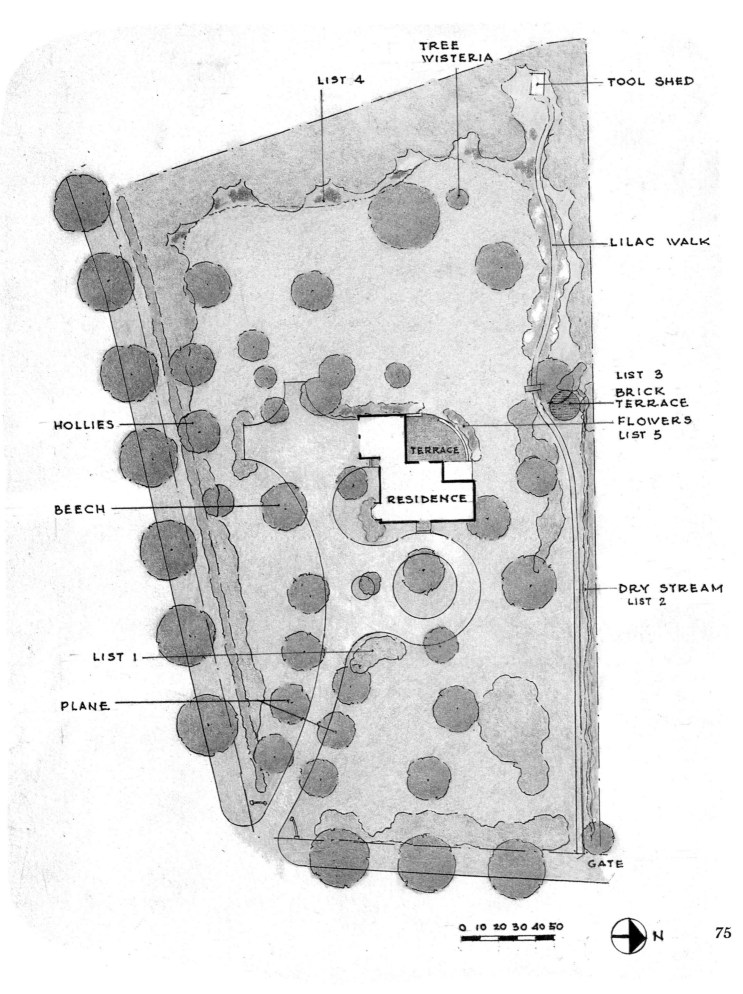

TREE
WISTERIA

LIST 4

TOOL SHED

LILAC WALK

LIST 3
BRICK
TERRACE
FLOWERS
LIST 5

HOLLIES

TERRACE

RESIDENCE

BEECH

DRY STREAM
LIST 2

LIST 1

PLANE

GATE

0 10 20 30 40 50

N

PART IV

Five to Ten Acres

This perennial garden backed by a cinderblock wall shows perennial candytuft as an edging and at this early stage clumps of lupines make a nice show. Beyond the garden wall a lilac path leads to a vegetable garden.

CHAPTER 10

A Flower-Lover's Many Gardens

On 6 acres overlooking one of the bays in Long Island Sound, an old stucco house built in the early 1900s has been lovingly restored and new gardens developed with many unusual plants. On my first visit in early winter I noticed the beautiful old trees, the position of the house and other buildings on the property and the spectacular water views. The only interesting feature in the landscape, however, was a honeysuckle arbor (*Lonicera japonica* 'Halliana') over the entranceway that gave fragrant blooms off and on all summer. The arbor makes a protected spot as a transition between the outside and inside and its perfume comes into the house—even as far as the upstairs bedrooms.

The owners wanted to add many things: a large terrace for entertaining, a perennial garden, a greenhouse, a tennis court, a swimming pool and a play area for children. My friend's interest in gardening is second only to her interest in her family; she enjoys working in the garden and knows every single plant on the property.

As often happens, these owners imagined developing their property with many different gardens. In this type of situation, I find that an overall master plan drawn up in the beginning is valuable. From the plan, the landscaping can be done in stages—the major "bones" first and other features as time passes. It can take several years to complete the plan, depending on how fast the owner wants to proceed. Many times it is best to move slowly in landscape development. People tend to get different ideas once they have lived

An arbor covered with 'Blaze' roses leads through to the herb garden.

The entrance to this home is completely enclosed by honeysuckle (Lonicera japonica 'Halliana'), a very fragrant and delightful approach in summer. Korean boxwoods line the wide walk.

The enclosed flower border shows pink and white columbines, lupines and daisies in bloom in late June.

in a new place for even a little while, and with a master plan, they can easily incorporate changes.

Soil and water conditions influence any garden plan, as they determine how things will grow. Here I discovered a very heavy clay subbase just 6 inches below the ground level. This clay held the water so plant roots could not develop properly. Two things were done—first I planned for drainage with underground tile drains. Second, almost all of the trees and shrubs were raised above the existing grade, providing a better soil foundation. Perennial roots grow down several feet; shrubs and trees, even deeper.

At the outset we decided to move the existing horseshoe-shaped gravel driveway farther from the gardener's cottage, providing more parking space and helping to keep strangers from driving in. The new layout of the driveway included a turnaround circling an old linden tree. In the spring, masses of daffodils bloom along the driveway.

One of the first features I planned was a large terrace and perennial garden on the south side of the house (list 1). The flower bed is adjacent to the terrace and porch and is framed by two very old plane trees (*Platanus occidentalis*). The property sloped 4½ feet to the south, so I had to level the ground in order to have the perennial garden on an even grade. I decided to enclose this garden with a stucco wall that matches the house. This protects the plants from the salt air and wind. The height of this wall was dictated by the fact that the owners wanted to see over it to the water beyond. The plants were all selected in shades of pink, white and blue. I anchored the ends of the perennial border with vitex (*Vitex Agnus-castus*), which makes a definite statement in the summer when the flowers bloom. The vines (*Clematis* varieties) trained over the walls have grown well and look like an old, established planting. On the far side of the wall, a few camellias have been planted and have survived the mild winters. They are protected in winter by a burlap fence.

I should point out that a few shrubs and vines add a lot to a perennial garden. They introduce different types of plant forms that have interest throughout the year, enhancing the structure of the garden. I have also found that perennial gardens benefit from a flexible approach; sometimes things work, sometimes they don't. Over the years, I have made changes in these perennial beds.

The perennial garden includes a small reflecting pool framed by roses and a holly hedge (*Ilex* ×*Meserveae* 'Blue Princess'). Roses were selected for their fragrance and long-blooming period (list 2). Outside of this garden on the bank, old-fashioned shrub roses have been used with a companion planting of Queen Anne's lace (*Daucus Carota*). The seeds were scattered over the ground in late fall, and the lovely white flowers bloomed the following year.

On the east side of the house a greenhouse serves as a dining area and spa, and is filled with many hardy indoor plants. I remember as I looked out from here one cold winter day the vivid contrast of the snow-covered landscape with frozen ornamental grasses outlined against the blue waters of the bay.

In an informal, woodsy area a little stream was built by the breakfast terrace just outside this greenhouse. I decided to build this stream because I thought it would be interesting to hear the sound of water close to the house. Even though the stream is man-made, it looks extremely natural. The stream meanders down the hill into a fish-filled pond, where a hidden terrace offers views of the bay beyond. This little stream is planted with a mixture of groundcovers and wildflowers (list 3) and has been enjoyed especially by the children who love to watch frogs and pollywogs as the water tumbles over the rocks. From the pond a path leads to the woodland trail that starts at the beach and wanders up the hill to the tennis court. Halfway up the trail there is a small gazebo, and numerous benches throughout this area provide places for enjoying the many varieties

Soft shades of early bloom and an abundance of new foliage herald spring around this woodland pool.

The wildflower walk through the woods shows early columbines, fritillaries, blue Scilla campanulata, bloodroots and bleeding hearts.

of wildflowers and summer-blooming, shade-loving perennials (list 4). At the end is a small pond with primroses.

The tennis court has a large terrace by the entrance and, across the court, its own gazebo, from which one can observe the players. The gazebo is above the level of the court, and the wide raised beds around it have been planted with buddleia and Korean boxwood—a nice combination for year-'round effect with little maintenance. The only necessary care is fertilizing once a year and cutting back the buddleia in the spring. The buddleia attracts butterflies all during the summer.

From the tennis court back toward the house the path runs alongside a beautiful stone wall filled with creeping and rock plants

Right:*Natural steps leading up to the tennis court with a dry stone wall are planted with* Phlox subulata. *This inexpensive little plant is easy to grow. A collection of daffodils and early tulips line the walk to the tennis court.*

(list 5) and interesting low-growing shrubs. A large lawn area for ball playing circles the driveway, and beyond it, an organic orchard of dwarf fruit trees. This is not a working orchard; no spraying is done. The fruit is picked, eaten and enjoyed by the family. This orchard is enclosed by a low-growing Belgian fence (see page 118 for a description of how a Belgian fence is constructed). Across the driveway, the gardener's cottage has a most interesting paved court-yard with bulbs, groundcovers and perennials set between the stones. A playhouse, a vegetable garden, an herb garden and a peony and lilac walk (list 6) are along the southern edge of the property. An old grape arbor behind the vegetable garden has been restored and now boasts many different varieties of vines.

Between the vegetable garden and the pool a curving path is planted with lilacs, peonies and St.-John's-wort (*Hypericum*), a summer-blooming shrub. A tree lilac (*Syringa amurensis*) also adds interest with its late bloom and stunning bark.

The swimming pool adjacent to the beach is a wonderful recreation area for everyone in the family, and it is here that a future pool house will be built. A gate toward the water leads to a dock and, just above, a stretch of lawn with a line of rocking chairs from which the view can be enjoyed.

Over the seven years that I have been working with these clients, their interest in and use of plants has increased tremendously. Their property has become a showcase for the Burpee product line of seeds and plants.

PLANT LIST

LIST 1 ❦ PERENNIAL GARDEN WITH PINKS, BLUES, WHITES

Achillea 'Galaxy' series (Yarrow)

Aconitum Napellus 'Sparks' (Monkshood)

Anemone hupehensis japonica 'September Charm' (Windflower)

Artemisia ludoviciana (Purlshiana) 'Silver King' (Wormwood, sagebrush)

Aster ×*Frikartii* (Aster, Michaelmas daisy)

Aster novae-angliae 'Harrington's Pink' (Aster)

Astilbe 'Amethyst' (Astilbe)

Astilbe 'Erica' (Astilbe)

Campanula calycanthema (Bellflower)

Campanula persicifolia (Bellflower)

Cimicifuga racemosa (Black snakeroot)

Dictamnus Fraxinella (Gas plant)

Gypsophila paniculata 'Bristol Fairy' (Baby's breath)

Lilium candidum (Madonna lily)

Lupinus 'Russell' Hybrids (Lupine)

Lythrum virgatum 'Morden Pink' (Lythrum)

Platycodon grandiflorus (Balloon flower)

Veronica spicata (Speedwell; blue)

LIST 2 ❦ ROSES BY A REFLECTING POOL

'Dainty Bess'

'Eclipse'

'The Fairy'

'Mr. Lincoln'

'Peace'

'Queen Elizabeth'

'Sea Foam'

LIST 3 ❦ WILDFLOWERS ALONG A STREAM

Astilbe (Astilbe; assorted)

Caltha palustris (Marsh marigold)

Cimicifuga simplex (Bugbane)

Hemerocallis (Daylily)
    June: 'Flavina' (soft yellow)
    July: 'Hyperion' (lemon yellow)
    August: 'Stella d'Oro' (gold)

Hosta, in variety (Plantain lily)

Iris Kaempferi (Japanese iris; deep purple, pink, white)

Iris Pseudacorus (Iris; yellow)

Iris sibirica (Iris; pinks and blues)

Primula japonica (Primrose)

Primula ×*polyantha* (Primrose)

Primula vulgaris (Primrose)

Groundcovers, Vines, Ferns and Grasses

Ajuga, in variety (Bugleweed)

Athyrium Filix-femina (Athyrium)

Dennstaedtia punctilobula (Cup fern)

Dryopteris marginalis (Leatherwood fern)

Galium odoratum (Sweet woodruff)

Hedera Helix 'Baltica' (Baltic ivy)

Hypericum calycinum (St.-John's-wort)

Liriope, in variety (Lilyturf)

Lysimachia Nummularia (Loosestrife)

Matteuccia pensylvanica (Ostrich fern)

Osmunda cinnamomea (Cinnamon fern)

Phalaris arundinacea picta (Ribbon grass)

Polystichum acrostichoides (Wood fern)

Viola, in variety (Violet)

Wisteria sinensis (Chinese wisteria)

LIST 4 ❦ WILDFLOWER GARDEN SHRUBS

Amelanchier canadensis (Shadblow)

Clethra alnifolia (Summer sweet)

Corylopsis spicata (Winter hazel)

Hamamelis virginiana (Common witch hazel)

Ilex glabra (Inkberry)

Ilex verticillata (Winterberry)

LIST 5 ❦ ROCK GARDEN

(Miniature and Small Plants to be Viewed up Close.)

Crocus 'Pickwick' (Crocus)

Crocus 'Yellow Giant' (Crocus)

Cyclamen, in variety (Persian violet)

Narcissus cyclamineus 'Jack Snipe' (Miniature daffodil)

Narcissus cyclamineus 'Tête à Tête' (Miniature daffodil)

Narcissus 'Thalia' (Miniature daffodil)

(continued)

(continued)

Nepeta ×*Faassenii* (Catmint)

Phlox subulata (Creeping phlox)

Saxifraga ×*Arendsii* 'Snow Carpet' (Rockfoil)

Sedum cauticolum (Stonecrop)

Thymus Serpyllum (Creeping thyme)

Thymus vulgaris 'Argenteus' (Golden lemon thyme)

Tulipa Clusiana (Tulip)

Tulipa Fosteriana 'Red Emperor' (Tulip)

Tulipa Kaufmanniana (Tulip)

Tulipa tarda (Tulip)

Viola 'Princess Blue' (Violet)

LIST 6 ❧ LILACS AND PEONIES

Lilacs

Syringa Meyeri 'Palibin'

Syringa patula 'Miss Kim'

Syringa ×*Prestoniae* 'James McFarlane'

Syringa villosa

Syringa vulgaris 'Katherine Havemeyer'

Syringa vulgaris 'Lucie Baltet'

Syringa vulgaris 'Ludwig Spaeth'

Syringa vulgaris 'Paul Thirion'

Peonies

Paeonia lactiflora 'Festiva Maxima'

Paeonia 'Le Cygne'

Paeonia 'Sarah Bernhardt'

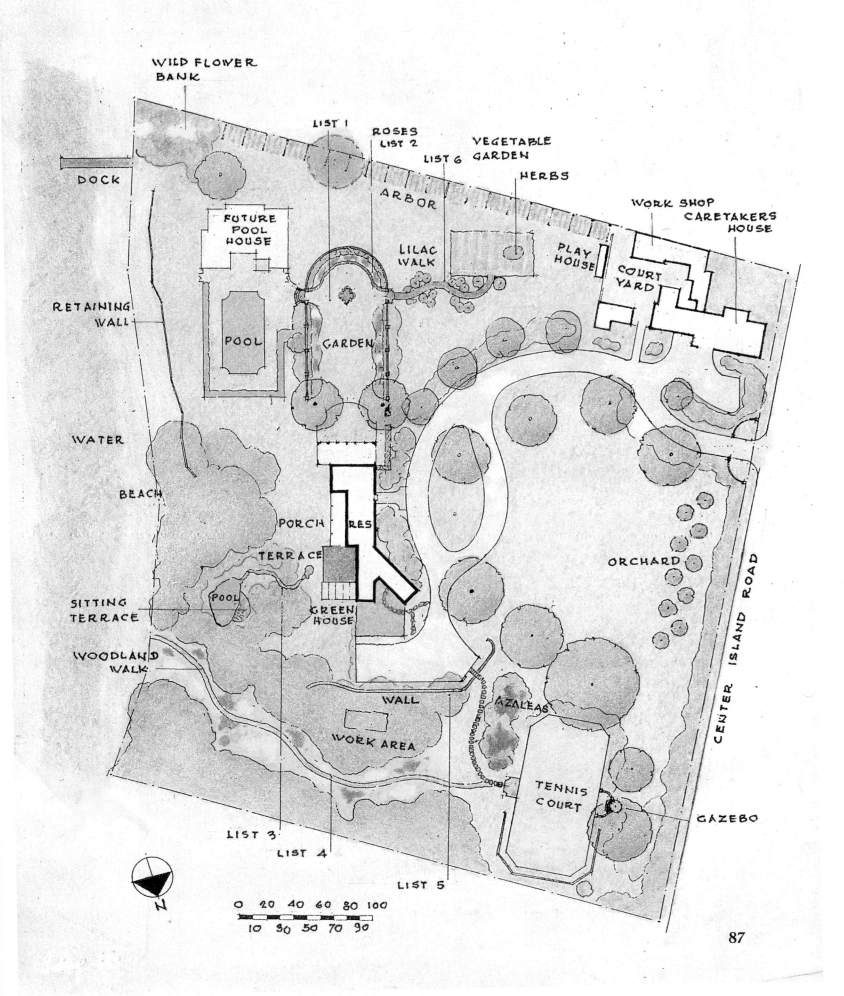

WILD FLOWER
BANK

DOCK

LIST 1

ROSES
LIST 2

LIST 6

VEGETABLE
GARDEN

HERBS

ARBOR

FUTURE
POOL
HOUSE

LILAC
WALK

WORK SHOP
CARETAKERS
HOUSE

PLAY
HOUSE

COURT
YARD

RETAINING
WALL

POOL

GARDEN

WATER

BEACH

PORCH   RES

ORCHARD

SITTING
TERRACE

TERRACE

POOL

GREEN
HOUSE

WOODLAND
WALK

WALL

AZALEAS

WORK AREA

CENTER ISLAND ROAD

TENNIS
COURT

GAZEBO

LIST 3

LIST 4

LIST 5

N

0   20   40   60   80   100
10   30   50   70   90

87

CHAPTER 11

A Stately
Home and Gardens

A colonial house set well back from a busy road on the New Jersey shore has been this family's home for many years. The client, with whom I have worked over a period of years, has always been involved in the local garden club and the Garden Club of America. She is a busy person, but spends much time and effort in her garden.

This 6-acre property was once surrounded by large estates. Eventually the open land was divided into house lots, which my clients felt made some enclosure necessary (list 1). The entrance to the house faces south. The wide path to the entry terrace and front door leads from a parking bay enclosed with lovely old holly trees and big yews. Japanese pagoda trees (*Sophora japonica*) frame the house, blooming in summer with panicles of white flowers. Chinese dogwood (*Cornus Kousa Chinensis*) flank the terrace and flower for several weeks in June. Beautiful lead containers, made to order, on each side of the front door are planted with espaliered osmanthus (*Osmanthus heterophyllus* 'Armatus') so they are a strong accent throughout the year. A beautiful flat-dish garden on the low wall serves as an exciting miniature garden.

On the east side with its old maple trees, a tall privet hedge hides the service drive. From the breakfast room and the enclosed porch, one looks out on a grassy area with old maple trees, some new holly trees, a beautiful lead fountain and a perennial border filled with white flowers (list 2). This wide border (7 × 60 feet) in front of the hedge is kept 3 feet away from the privet, allowing space for

White perennial candytuft 'White Admiral', 'Mt. Tacoma' tulips and white bleeding hearts accent this all-white flower garden in early spring.

*The front entrance to this home is planted with longstalk holly (*Ilex pedunculosa*) and 'Delaware Valley White' azaleas.*

This container garden placed on the entrance wall and filled with sedum, rockcress, draba, bluet and thyme is interesting to look at all through the year.

maintenance. The all-white border includes a variety of plants, which bloom continually throughout the summer. It is a lovely sight from early May, when the white 'Mt. Tacoma' tulips and white bleeding hearts bloom together. Bleeding heart is an old favorite of mine; interestingly, *Dicentra spectabilis* disappears almost entirely by mid-July, but the low-growing *D. eximia* continues to bloom throughout the summer. Holly trees enclose this area and frame the recently installed fountain. The birds enjoy it, and the sound of dripping water is a lovely addition on hot summer days. An existing old Japanese maple ends the perennial border and is a beautiful sight in fall when its leaves turn a lovely bronze color. White gardens are often referred to as "moon gardens." They can be very romantic, visually, as the moonlight shining on the white blossoms gives them an almost iridescent quality. Add the fragrance of many of the white flowers, and you have a most appealing garden.

To the west of the house, a Japanese garden has evolved (list 3). Japanese gardens in America are quite different from gardens in Japan, but I feel that they have a place in our landscape—most particularly when they can be designed as a separate area. In this case, the yew hedges and interesting fence at the back give the area an enclosed feeling. As one enters the garden through a wooden gate, on one side is a dwarf Japanese maple and on the other side a Japanese pagoda tree.

This was once a flat area with a rectangular pool and a rose garden; before that it had been a perennial garden. Most recently, by raising the grade three feet along the walk an appropriately Japanese feeling of movement was produced. This walk leads to a Japanese white pine (*Pinus parviflora*). Beneath this cotoneasters, dwarf azaleas (*Rhododendron Satsuki*) 'Azalea Gumpo' and *R. mucronatum* 'Delaware Valley White' are planted. The walk descends again into a shady area that is planted with *Euonymus alatas* and gives the feeling of walking through a small woodland. The burning bush has to be

*A dwarf pine (*Pinus parviflora*) is the accent tree in this Japanese garden with its little rock pool. Creeping juniper is used as a groundcover. Euonymus alata, the burning bush, provides nice autumn color and a woodland feeling.*

The gazebo at the end of the garden is flanked with flowering dogwood, dwarf beech trees and English boxwoods. Later in the season the urns are filled with pale pink geraniums, which bloom throughout the summer.

pruned regularly, but has brilliant fall foliage and winged branches that hold the snow in winter—a lovely sight.

The alignment of the pool was changed with rocks and a waterfall. Creeping plants climb over the sides of the pool and a bronze crab bought in Japan perches on the edge. These plants are *Cotoneaster apiculatus, Juniperus communis* 'Hornibrookii', *J. procumbens* 'Nana' and *J. Sargentii* 'Glauca'.

This whole garden is enclosed in a planting of *Malus* Hybrid 'Red Jade', *Magnolia grandiflora* and some English hollies. There is a delightful sitting spot at the rear from which you can gaze back at the little waterfall pool. The entire area is restful and serene, truly the feeling of a Japanese garden.

From the existing terrace with its sitting wall, one can look into the Japanese garden and also get a lovely view of the length of the property to the delicate gazebo at the far end. The gazebo is surrounded by boxwoods and flanked at the entrance by two dwarf weeping beeches (*Fagus sylvatica* 'Purpurea Pendula'), beyond which are old dogwoods (*Cornus florida*). In summer, hanging baskets of geraniums add a nice touch to this quiet sitting spot.

Between the gazebo and the Japanese garden is a collection of flowering trees and large shrubs that we planted to screen the development of new houses. This planting includes hollies (*Ilex opaca*) for winter effect. The flowering trees have a sequence of bloom beginning with the crab apples (*Malus floribunda*), then the silver bells (*Halesia carolina*), next the fringe trees (*Chionanthus virginicus*) and last the Washington hawthorns (*Crataegus Phaenopyrum*). The hawthorns are particularly nice in winter, for they keep their berries late into the season. Opposite this planting are three Goldenrain trees (*Koelreuteria paniculata*), which bloom in summer with yellow blossoms and interesting seed pods. Here also are masses of lilacs (*Syringa* Hybrids), which the owner enjoys cutting for bouquets in her home. Beneath these flowering trees and shrubs a future planting of hollies and rhododendron is planned.

This lovely property with wonderful old trees and large open spaces still provides many opportunities for the additional gardens that the owner plans. Large or small, a garden is truly never finished.

PLANT LIST

LIST 1 ❧ SCREEN/ENCLOSURE PLANTING

Cedrus atlantica 'Glauca' (Blue atlas cedar)

Chionanthus virginicus (Fringe tree)

Crataegus Phaenopyrum (Washington hawthorn)

Halesia carolina (Silver bell tree)

Ilex opaca (American holly)

Koelreuteria paniculata (Goldenrain tree)

Malus floribunda (Flowering crabapple)

LIST 2 ❧ WHITE FLOWER BORDER

Achillea ×*Lewisii* 'King Edward' (Yarrow)

Achillea Ptarmica 'The Pearl' (Yarrow)

Anemone japonica (Windflower)

Aquilegia flabellata 'Alba' (Columbine)

Aster novi-belgii 'Snowflurry' (Aster, Michaelmas daisy)

Astilbe ×*Ardensii* 'Deutschland' (Astilbe)

Astilbe Thunbergi 'Professor Weilen' (Astilbe)

Campanula persicifolia 'Grand Alba' (Bellflower)

Delphinium × *Belladonna* Hybrid (Delphinium; white varieties)

Dicentra eximia (Wild bleeding heart)

Dicentra spectabilis (Bleeding heart)

Dictamnus albus (Gas plant)

Digitalis purpurea 'Alba' (Foxglove)

Gypsophila paniculata 'Perfecta' (Baby's breath)

Miscanthus sinensis 'Gracillimus' (Grass)

Heuchera sanguinea 'White Cloud' (Coralbells)

Hosta elegance (Plantain lily)

Hosta grandiflora (Plantain lily)

Hosta Sieboldiana (Plantain lily)

Iberis sempervirens 'Autumn Beauty' (Candytuft)

Iris 'Fourfold White' (Iris)

Iris Kaempferi 'Gold Bound' (Iris)

Iris 'Lady in Waiting' (Iris)

Iris sibirica 'Snow Queen' (Siberian iris)

Iris 'Silver Shower' (Bearded iris)

Iris 'Symphony' (Iris)

Iris 'White Wedgwood' (Iris)

Lilium auratum (Lily)

Lilium 'Casa Blanca' (Lily)

Lilium 'Imperial Silver' (Lily)

Lilium regale (Regal lily)

Lilium speciosum album (Lily)

Lupinus 'Russell' Hybrids (Lupine)

Paeonia 'Bowl of Cream' (Peony)

Paeonia 'Charles White' (Peony)

Paeonia lactiflora 'Festiva Maxima' (Peony)

Paeonia 'Miss America' (Peony)

Papaver orientale 'Barr's White' (Oriental poppy)

Papaver orientale 'Marshall von der Goltz' (Oriental poppy)

Phlox carolina 'Miss Lingard' (Phlox)

Phlox paniculata 'White Admiral' (Phlox)

Platycodon grandiflorus 'Albus' (Balloon flower)

Stokesia laevis 'Alba' (Stoke's aster)

Tulipa 'Mt. Tacoma' (Tulip)

Veronica alpina 'Alba' (Speedwell)

Veronica longifolia subsessile (Speedwell)

Veronica spicata 'Icicle' (Speedwell)

LIST 3 ❧ JAPANESE GARDEN

Cotoneaster horizontalis (Rockspray cotoneaster)

Euonymus alata (Burning bush)

Ilex pedunculosa (Longstalk holly)

Pinus parviflora (Japanese white pine)

Styrax japonica (Japanese snowbell)

Rhododendron Satsuki (Azalea gumpo)

Rhododendron mucronatum 'Delaware Valley White' (Azalea)

Creeping Plants

Cotoneaster apiculatus (Cranberry cotoneaster)

Juniperus communis 'Hornibrookii' (Common juniper)

Juniperus procumbens 'Nana' (Juniper)

Juniperus Sargentii 'Glauca' (Blue Sargent juniper)

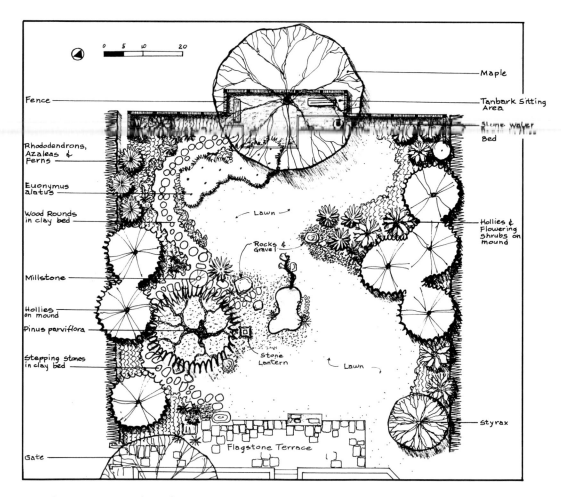

Detail: Japanese Garden (list 3).

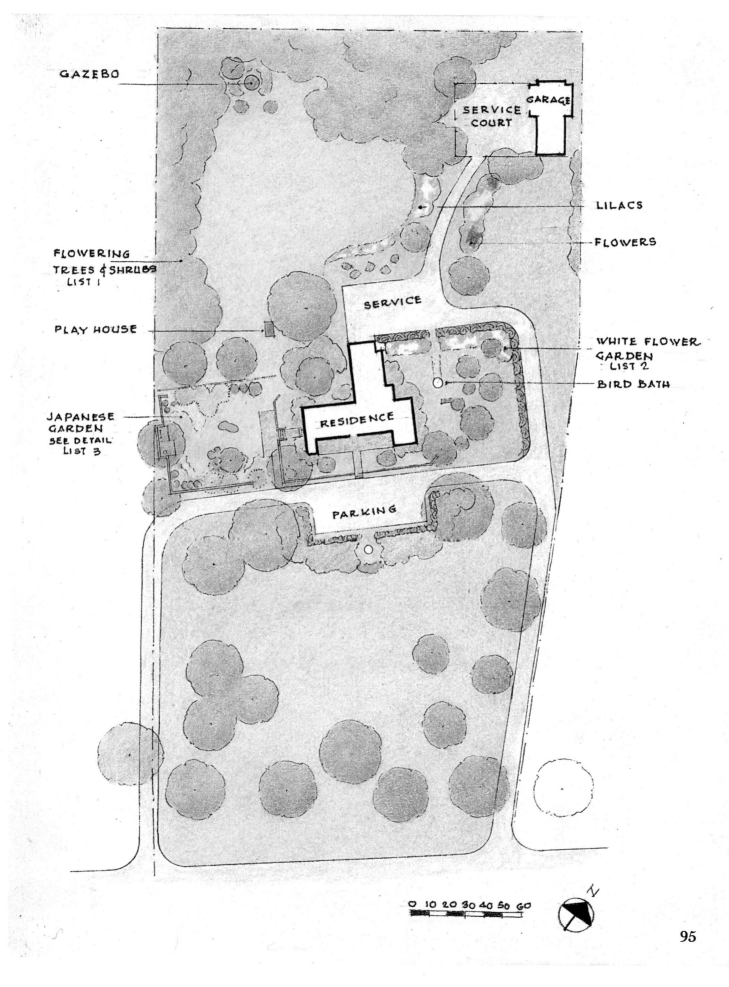

GAZEBO

SERVICE
COURT

GARAGE

LILACS

FLOWERS

FLOWERING
TREES & SHRUBS
LIST 1

SERVICE

PLAY HOUSE

WHITE FLOWER
GARDEN
LIST 2

BIRD BATH

RESIDENCE

JAPANESE
GARDEN
SEE DETAIL
LIST 3

PARKING

0 10 20 30 40 50 60

N

CHAPTER 12

Gardens for a Waterfront Home

Some 25 years ago when my client and I first walked on this land, it was a 5-acre potato field with hedgerows along each side of the property. There was a lovely view of the water. We discussed where the house should be placed to best take advantage of the views of a creek and the ocean beyond. We also wanted to provide special features in the landscape, including a pool and gardens. A driveway and spacious courtyard for 10 cars were required at the outset. In subsequent years we have added a tennis court, garage/greenhouse and paths alongside the wide perimeter plantings along with many other new plantings.

The long, curving driveway has been lined with apple trees (*Malus* 'Red Delicious' and 'Yellow Transparency') selected primarily for their lovely shape. The habit of these two varieties is the same, and I thought it would be nice to have two different kinds of apples. Some trees have been blown over in recent hurricanes, but they were quickly righted and guyed with wire to hold them in place, and they have survived.

Entrance courtyards are a favorite feature of mine—they are extremely necessary and, although they are unfortunately so often unattractive, they can be perfectly lovely. This one has a center island highlighted with a swamp red maple (*Acer rubrum*) surrounded by a Korean boxwood hedge (*Buxus microphylla koreana*). Planted with pink impatiens, the island helps make the entrance courtyard a

Looking through an allée of Kwanzan cherry trees toward the pool enclosed with a picket fence and two boxwoods at the entrance.

The front entrance with the swamp red maple in the circle has large boxwoods on each side· of the front door flanked by Cryptomeria. *Along each colonnade, pink roses repeat the pink color of the impatiens within the boxwood edging.*

beautiful and welcoming sight throughout the summer. The 8-foot flagstone walk is unusually wide, but it provides a gracious path to the broad front door. A pair of tall *Cryptomeria japonica* 'Lobbii' and boxwood (*B. sempervirens*) complete the entrance planting (list 1). Along the colonnades that flank the entry path, roses with an edging of sweet alyssum add color and fragrance all summer; boxwood behind the roses adds interest in winter. Clematis have been planted at posts along these walks—*Clematis Henryi* with its white blossoms, and the pure white *C. candidum.*

Terraces with sitting walls encircle the house on the west and overlook the water. Tubs of potted plants—plumbagos and geraniums— are used on each side of the sliding doors opening out from the plant room. A balcony above repeats these plantings. The dining terrace has a lattice trellis on the wall with morning glories. Fairy roses (*Rosa polyantha* 'The Fairy') have been planted below the sitting walls to give continuous summer bloom; they require a minimum amount of care and thrive without spraying. Two large plane trees (*Platanus occidentalis*) that were planted when the terrace was built now give ample shade and frame the house. A pair of lions and matched dwarf cypress (*Chamaecyparis obtusa* 'Nana') guard wide steps down to the open lawn. This lawn has adequate space for large gatherings and is level enough to tent on special occasions. At the edge of the water, daylilies, salt-spray roses (*Rosa rugosa*) and mallows (*Hibiscus Moscheutos*) bloom throughout the summer. One old, wild crab apple

'Golden Showers' roses on the pool fence bloom almost continuously throughout the summer.

(*Malus baccata*) has matured nicely at the water's edge and another has recently been added to screen the view of a house across the creek.

The swimming pool is reached through an allée of Kwanzan cherries (*Prunus serrulata* 'Kwanzan') and pink impatiens. Although the cherry blossoms come in May and are gone by the swimming season, the trees' shape and growth habit make them ideal for an allée planting. The pool is surrounded by a low brick wall topped by a white picket fence covered with *Rosa* 'New Dawn' climbing roses. Outside of the wall, a grove of white birches (*Betula alba*) circles the area and their silhouettes give a light, airy effect. Between the birches and the wall, a 6-foot-wide flower bed with boxwood at 20-foot intervals has recently been made into a summer garden, filled with colorful annuals. The pool pavilion has mirrors that reflect the water and garden beyond.

Adjacent to the garage and greenhouse is a walled cutting garden where masses of flowers for the house are planted. The wall protects the plants from rabbits and other animals and, in addition, creates a warm spot for seedlings to flourish. Meidiland roses (*Rosa* 'Bonica') and boxwood soften the outside face of the wall.

To plant along the north property line and driveway the owner selected a combination of iris that she loves. This is a joy to see in June (list 2). Behind these iris a flagstone walk meanders through a collection of summer-blooming plants (list 3). They are backed by evergreens (list 4).

The cutting garden beside the garage is enclosed with a wall and a picket fence. Cosmos, zinnias, daisies and ageratum are growing here in profusion. The espaliered pear tree against the garage will eventually bear fruit.

Along the south side adjacent to the street, a planting of summer-blooming perennials has been added. Astilbes in various shades of pink bloom throughout June and July. The large leaves of *Ligularia stenocephala* 'The Rocket' fill the corner; the blossoms are stunning in July.

Island plantings have been used to direct attention to various points on the property. Islands filled with birch, weigelas, abelias, astilbe, inkberries, blue vitex, caryopteris, hydrangeas and clethra mark the approach to the tennis court. The islands also serve to break up the large lawn so that you don't see everything at once. Some annuals are added each year to give additional color (list 5).

Roses are another of the owner's favorite flowers. I have used many different varieties in locations scattered throughout the property. There are hybrid teas on each side of the colonnade and along the approach to the front door, 'The Fairy' rose below the main terrace and along the dining terrace, climbing roses around the swimming pool and old-fashioned roses by the brick wall around the cutting garden.

This home is primarily used in the summer, and there is always something blooming on this property, June through September. The client loves flowers and is anxious to have many varieties included in the gardens, borders along the property lines and the five island plantings. However, even in winter there is something attractive to see. Brick walls and piers topped with lead geese frame

An iris walk along the property line shows the Siberian iris in full bloom in early July.

The island planting here has impatiens and pachysandra as an edging, backed by the burning bush, leucothoe and hydrangea. A shadblow tree and a white pine give accent in the center.

wooden gates at the entrance to the curving driveway. The apple trees, which have matured so nicely, mark a sweeping avenue to the front door. Surrounded by a blanket of snow, they give an expectant feeling of all that is to come when the first signs of spring appear.

PLANT LIST

LIST 1 ❧ ENTRANCE COURTYARD

Acer rubrum (Red maple)

Buxus microphylla koreana (Korean boxwood)

Buxus sempervirens (Boxwood)

Cladrastis lutea (American yellow-wood)

Cryptomeria japonica 'Lobbii' (Japanese cedar)

Picea Abies (Norway spruce)

Rhododendron Hybrid 'Scintillation' (Rhododendron)

Taxus ×*media* 'Hatfieldii' (Yew hedge)

Tilia cordata (Little-leaf linden)

LIST 2 ❧ IRIS

Iris sibirica (Siberian iris; narrow, grass-like foliage requires moist, fertile, slightly acid soil)

'Navy Brass'

'Reddy Maid'

'Sky Wings'

'White Sails'

Iris Kaempferi (Japanese iris; requires sun, rich soil, no lime)

'Favorite'

'Frosted Fountain'

'Moonlight Waves'

'Pink Lady'

'Royal Banner'

Iris (Bearded iris; requires full sun, well-drained soil)

'Apricot Beauty'

'Arctic Fury'

'Blue Sapphire'

'Dutch Chocolate'

'Jessie Viette'

'Night Owl'

'Pink Beauty'

'Sapphire Hills'

'Southern Comfort'

LIST 3 ❧ PLANTS ALONG WALK BEHIND IRIS

Achillea Hybrid 'Moonshine' (Yarrow)

Aconitum Fischeri (Monkshood)

Amsonia ciliata (Amsonia)

Anchusa azurea (Anchusa)

Anthemis tinctoria (Chamomile)

Asclepias tuberosa (Butterfly weed)

Boltonia asteroides (Boltonia)

Chelone Lyonii (Turtlehead)

Cimicifuga simplex (Bugbane)

Eupatorium coelestinum (Hardy ageratum)

Hyssopus officinalis (Hyssop)

Lobelia siphilitica (Lobelia)

Lysimachia clethroides (Gooseneck)

Perovskia atriplicifolia (Russian sage)

Primula Hybrids (Primrose)

Salvia azurea grandiflora (Sage)

Tricyrtis hirta (Japanese toad lily)

Yucca filamentosa (Adam's needle yucca)

LIST 4 ❧ EVERGREEN PLANTING

Chamaecyparis obtusa 'Nana' (Hinoki cypress)

×*Cupressocyparis Leylandii* (Leyland cypress)

Ilex opaca (American holly)

Picea Omorika (Serbian spruce)

Rhododendron maximum (Rosebay rhododendron)

LIST 5 ❧ ISLAND PLANTING— (These islands vary in size from 20 × 10 feet to 30 × 15 feet.)

Abelia ×*grandiflora* (Abelia)

Caryopteris 'Blue Mist' (Blue spirea)

Clethra alnifolia (Summersweet)

Hibiscus syriacus 'Banner' (Rose mallow)

Hydrangea macrophylla 'Nikko Blue' (Hydrangea)

Ilex glabra (Inkberry)

Ilex ×*Meserveae* (Blue holly)

Ilex verticillata (Winterberry)

Leucothoe Fontanesiana (Drooping leucothoe)

Vitex Agnus-castus 'Latifolia' (Chaste tree)

Weigela Hybrid 'Eva Supreme' (Weigela)

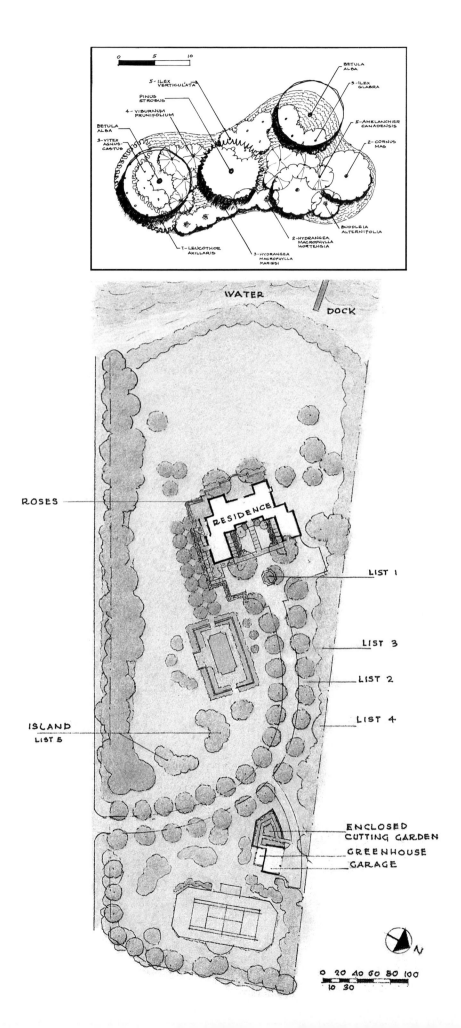

0   5   10

5- ILEX
VERTICULATA

PINUS
STROBUS

4- VIBURNUM
PRUNIFOLIUM

BETULA
ALBA

3- VITEX
AGNUS-
CASTUS

BETULA
ALBA

3- ILEX
GLABRA

5- AMELANCHIER
CANADENSIS

2- CORNUS
MAS

BUDDLEIA
ALTERNIFOLIA

2- HYDRANGEA
MACROPHYLLA
HORTENSIA

3- HYDRANGEA
MACROPHYLLA
MARISSI

7- LEUCOTHOE
AXILLARIS

WATER

DOCK

ROSES

RESIDENCE

LIST 1

LIST 3

LIST 2

LIST 4

ISLAND
LIST 5

ENCLOSED
CUTTING GARDEN
GREENHOUSE
GARAGE

N

0 20 40 60 80 100
   10   30

PART V

Ten Acres and More

The Belgian fence makes an interesting separation between six little gardens. A wide grass path leads to the center axis where dwarf boxwood surrounds a star magnolia.

CHAPTER 13

A Remodeled
Farm and Gardens

This stately brick house overlooks open fields where horses once roamed. Now it is the home of a couple and their large family, who enjoy an active life on the lovely rolling acres. The new owners wanted an attractive layout that would include new plantings in the entrance courtyard, terraces for entertaining both small and large groups, a terrace under an existing beech tree near the kitchen for family cooking and dining, a pool with a pool house and a variety of gardens for year-'round interest. The property is surrounded by woods and open meadows that are often used by the local hunt club. The land is inhabited by a large number of deer, which the owners enjoy. There were very few existing trees around the house, so I planted a number of large shade trees, some big hollies and a collection of flowering trees (list 1).

Entering this 10-acre property from the main road, the drive winds through stone piers and up a hill. A post-and-rail fence has been installed on both sides of the road and crab apple trees (*Malus* 'Katherine') are planted along the way. 'New Dawn' roses climb the fence posts. A glimpse of the house is visible as one proceeds through a woodland, where hemlocks and rhododendron have been planted among the existing old trees. The drive then runs through a dogwood allée (*Cornus Kousa Chinensis*), and passes under an arch into a large, brick-paved courtyard.

The entrance court features a beautiful lead urn filled with seasonal flowers. Flowers are planted around the urn as well, so

A perennial garden filled with phlox, Aster ×Frikartii and daisies in summer bloom frames a pastoral scene.

The center island with an old urn has been planted with red and white impatiens for summer color. Dwarf cypress and 'Delaware Valley White' azaleas along with an edging of dwarf boxwoods have been used as the foundation planting.

there is always something attractive to look at; bulbs are planted for spring, wax begonias for summer and chrysanthemums for fall. Dwarf cypress (*Chamaecyparis obtusa* 'Gracilis') grow on either side of the front door. In the borders around the house, 'Delaware Valley White' azaleas, 'Windbeam' rhododendron and 'Blue Princess' hollies thrive in beds of *Vinca minor* along with an edging of dwarf boxwoods (*Buxus microphylla koreana*). Two honey locust trees (*Gleditsia triacanthos* 'Halka') planted in the corners frame the building. This fast-growing variety holds its leaves well into the fall, then has the desirable habit of dropping them all at once (list 2).

The open porch that extends the length of the house looks down on the meadow, facing a well-traveled country road. This road is hidden by old white pines. I added some new ones, and a mass of flowering dogwood for their spring bloom and fall foliage. Because the family entertains frequently, it was essential that the area in front of the porch be level and open to provide space for tents. Three Zelkova trees were planted at the far edge of this level area. As these trees mature they look like the American elm, so they will eventually frame the view from the porch.

At the end of the porch beneath an old beech tree, there is a terrace that was recently enlarged. It has an interesting pool with an

The family uses this terrace for dining. An old beech tree has a lovely English bench surrounding it. Next to the house a dwarf Japanese maple gives a touch of color.

unusual waterfall quite visible from the kitchen window. A beautiful limestone bench brought from England surrounds the old beech tree, making a pleasant spot to sit and look out over the meadow. The adjacent cutting garden features shade-loving, flowering plants (list 3).

At the opposite end of the house an octagonal terrace off the living room has two Japanese maples that frame a view of the farm buildings and orchard. There is a lovely feeling of being surrounded by greenery. The gazebo-like pool house at the end is a focal point for family entertaining. Because this is well below the house, enclosed with flowering trees and shrubs, it enjoys complete privacy. The pool equipment area is protected by a bamboo planting that not only hides the machinery, but cuts down on the noise as well. (The bamboo is cut back to 6 feet several times during the summer.) There is a wide walk underneath an old apple tree up to a cottage adjacent to the house. Another walk has been created from the octagonal terrace under a Goldenrain tree (*Koelreuteria paniculata*). Masses of roses are planted along this upper walk.

To the north of the house is a sunken perennial garden (list 4). Its circular path surrounds an open lawn. A wide flower border along the outside of the path is filled with perennials and annuals for continuous summer bloom. A gazebo opposite the steps makes a

Off of the dining terrace, this little cascading pool gives a pleasant sound. Leucothoe is planted around the top of the pool for winter interest.

Rhododendron 'Scintillation' blooming near the house. The pool house is in the distance beneath the branches of the maple.

pleasant space to pause and look back. (This part of the garden was constructed and planted in just three months, in order to be ready for a large family wedding in the late summer.)

The drive to the farm buildings down the hill passes a row of Sargent crab apples. These dwarf trees were particularly selected so one could look over them and see the fields beyond. The drive then goes through an old orchard. New apple trees have recently been added. Near the barns, a large vegetable garden supplies not only the family but also the neighbors.

This swimming pool area with its gazebo-type pool house is surrounded by roses, potted plants and one weeping cherry tree.

A brick path encircling the perennial garden in full summer bloom.

The existing barns are now used for sheep, goats, a cow, a bull, lots of chickens, pot-bellied pigs and a donkey family. Handsome peacocks roam the property, and white and black Australian swans plus four different varieties of ducks can be found on the pond. Today, the growing family enjoys the farm on frequent occasions—from family parties and weddings, to benefits, home and garden tours and groups of schoolchildren. The owners are most generous in sharing their beautiful country home with many who love to come and enjoy the lovely open, rolling lands.

PLANT LIST

LIST 1 ❧ TREES

Cedrus atlantica (Atlas cedar)

Ginkgo biloba (Maidenhair tree)

Gleditsia triacanthos 'Halka' (Honey locust)

Ilex Aquifolium 'Nellie R. Stevens' (English holly)

Ilex opaca (American holly)

Juglans nigra (Black walnut)

Koelreuteria paniculata (Goldenrain tree)

Magnolia stellata (Star magnolia)

Malus Sargentii (Sargent crab apple)

Pyrus Calleryana 'Bradford' (Bradford pear)

Zelkova serrata (Zelkova)

LIST 2 ❧ ENTRANCE COURT

Betula populifolia (Common birch)

Buxus microphylla koreana (Korean dwarf boxwood)

Buxus sempervirens 'Suffruticosa' (Boxwood)

Chamaecyparis obtusa 'Gracilis' (Dwarf cypress)

Ginkgo biloba (Maidenhair tree)

Gleditsia triacanthos 'Halka' (Honey locust)

Ilex ×*Meserveae* 'Blue Princess' (Blue holly)

Rhododendron mucronatum 'Delaware Valley White' (Azalea)

Rhododendron 'Windbeam' (Rhododendron)

LIST 3 ❧ SHADY CUTTING GARDEN

Anemone japonica (Windflower)

Chrysogonum virginianum (Golden star)

Cimicifuga simplex (Bugbane)

Coreopsis 'Moonbeam' (Coreopsis)

Eupatorium coelestinum (Mist flower)

Geranium sanguineum 'Album' (Perennial geranium)

Iris sibirica (Siberian iris)

Lobelia siphilitica (Lobelia)

Monarda didyma (Bee balm)

Salvia azurea (Sage)

Tricyrtis hirta (Toad lily)

Veronica spicata 'Icicle' (Speedwell)

LIST 4 ❧ PERENNIAL GARDEN

Abelia ×*grandiflora* (Abelia)

Achillea Hybrid 'Moonshine' (Yarrow)

Achillea 'Red Beauty' (Yarrow)

Aconitum Carmichaelii (Fischeri) (Monkshood)

Anemone japonica 'Alba' (Windflower)

Anemone japonica 'Rosea' (Windflower)

Aquilegia chrysantha (Columbine)

Aster ×*Frikartii* (Aster, Michaelmas daisy)

Aster novae-angliae 'Harrington's Pink' (Aster)

Astilbe ×*Arendsii* 'Deutschland' (Astilbe)

Campanula persicifolia 'Alba' (Bellflower)

Cimicifuga simplex 'White Pearl' (Bugbane)

Delphinium Pacific Giant Hybrids 'Belladonna' (Delphinium)

Delphinium Pacific Giant Hybrids 'Casa Blanca' (Delphinium)

Dictamnus albus (Gas plant)

Dictamnus purpureus (Gas plant)

Digitalis purpurea 'Excelsior Mixed' (Foxglove)

Doronicum cordatum (caucasicum) 'Mme. Mason' (Leopard's-bane)

Gypsophila paniculata 'Bristol Fairy' (Baby's breath)

Heuchera sanguinea 'June Bride' (Coralbells)

Iberis sempervirens 'Snowflake' (Candytuft)

Iris, bearded, selected varieties (Iris)

Lupinus 'Russell' Hybrids (Lupine)

Lythrum virgatum 'Morden Pink' (Loosestrife)

Monarda didyma 'Croftway Pink' (Bee balm)

Paeonia 'Alsace Lorraine' (Peony)

Paeonia 'Baroness Schroeder' (Peony)

Paeonia 'Frances Wellard' (Peony)

Paeonia lactiflora 'Festiva Maxima' (Peony)

Paeonia 'Kelway's Glorious' (Peony)

Paeonia 'Krinkled White' (Peony)

Paeonia 'Le Cygne' (Peony)

Paeonia 'Mrs. Frank Beach' (Peony)
Paeonia 'Perry's White' (Peony)
Paeonia 'Rosy Dawn' (Peony)
Paeonia 'Sarah Bernhardt' (Peony)
Paeonia 'Solange' (Peony)
Paeonia suffruticosa (Tree peony)
Papaver orientale 'Beauty of Livermore' (Oriental poppy)
Papaver orientale 'Bonfire' (Oriental poppy)
Papaver orientale 'Helen Elizabeth' (Oriental poppy)
Papaver orientale 'Mrs. Perry' (Oriental poppy)
Phlox carolina 'Miss Lingard' (Phlox)

Phlox decussata 'White Admiral' (Phlox)
Phlox paniculata 'Bright Eyes' (Phlox)
Phlox paniculata 'Dresden China' (Phlox)
Platycodon grandiflorus 'Albus' (Balloon flower)
Platycodon grandiflorus 'Mariesii' (Balloon flower)
Scabiosa caucasica 'House Mixture' (Scabious, pincushion flower)
Sedum spectabile 'Autumn Joy' (Stonecrop)
Stokesia laevis 'Blue Moon' (Stokes' aster)
Veronica spicata 'Blue Peter' (Speedwell)

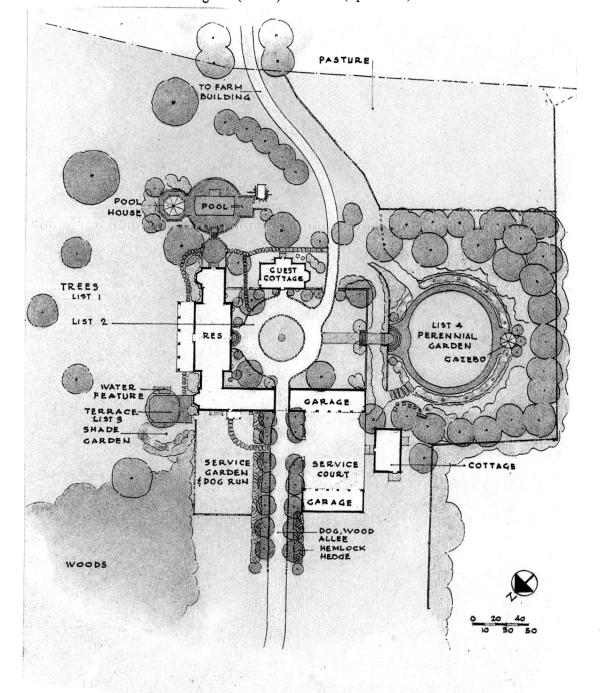

CHAPTER 14

Many Gardens for a Farmhouse

A remodeled old farmhouse on 20 acres is situated on a gently rolling hill near Princeton, New Jersey, overlooking an old canal. Over the years the owners had altered the house for a large family, rebuilt the barn and developed the farmland for cattle. Now the time had come to design the garden of their dreams. Before I arrived, the front of the house that overlooked the canal—as well as a road—had been the focus of their attention. Now, with an increase in road traffic, they decided to turn their back on this area and begin to address the land between the house and the pasture.

On my first visit we sat on a small terrace that overlooked a lawn enclosed with a hemlock hedge. Beyond the hedge, cows were grazing. We discussed what the owners wanted and the possibilities of the site. Both clients were intensely interested in plants. The husband had grown up nearby, in a family that loved gardens; he was primarily concerned with the structure and design of the garden. His Australian wife is a knowledgeable plantswoman and wanted many varieties of perennials included in a series of small gardens. They knew that they would like to include a terrace and a swimming pool, along with an interesting collection of trees and shrubs.

The first order of business was to resolve the issues that interested the husband the most—namely, the plan. We often disagreed on the exact placement of many things, but discussions were always constructive and the results pleased everyone.

A terrace overlooks an elegant pool area and, in the background, a more rustic pasture.

Okame cherry trees bloom early, have lovely fall color and grow very fast. Rhododendron are planted beneath these trees.

A large flagstone terrace has space for entertaining. The wisteria arbor protects the walk to the back door and the Viburnum tomentosum *fills the space beneath the big window.*

The view from the terrace of the barn and a hemlock hedge that encircles the garden.

116

The long drive that runs along the property line had old evergreen trees that were removed and replaced with a double row (30 in all) of Okame cherries (*Prunus Okame*). These trees grow quickly, have lovely pink blossoms and display good fall color. They are underplanted with hybrid rhododendron ('Boule de Neige', 'Mrs. C. S. Sargent', Hybrid 'Scintillation') and native azaleas (*Rhododendron Vaseyi, R. viscosum, R. nudiflorum, R. Schlippenbachii*). Beyond the cherries is a view to an old farm pond.

Approaching the front door of the house from the side beneath an existing long, wisteria-covered arbor, one sees the large terrace, a perfect setting for parties. The main section of terrace is some 60 feet long, which is large enough to accommodate 50 guests. A raised section was added a few years ago with easy access to the kitchen to facilitate serving family meals.

Beyond the terrace a lovely open area with old trees is enclosed by a hemlock hedge that has been allowed to grow to 10 feet—just the right height to be able to see over it to fields and cows in the distance. Walking from the terrace into this open area, one sees a raised gazebo in one corner. But entering the garden, a wonderful surprise awaits you.

The gazebo in the corner of the hemlock hedge looks out over six little gardens as well as a corner of the pool. This perennial garden has white flowers.

The Belgian fence surrounding each garden was started when the gardens were first constructed. It makes a lovely enclosure as well as producing flowers in spring and pears in the late summer.

Six beautiful little gardens are laid out in an enclosed area that is a little larger than a tennis court. Each garden is different, and all have narrow paths of crushed local stone. The first gardens seen are for herbs and roses, and then there are four perennial gardens, each enclosed by a Belgian fence of pear trees. The fence is a type of espalier—a variation of the single horizontal cordon, in which the branches of fruit trees are trained on wire in opposite 45-degree angles to form a lattice or diamond-shaped pattern. This type of fence is particularly good for separating different sections of a large garden, because it is truly part of the garden. It has an interesting form in the winter, is lovely in spring, bears fruit in summer and has nice fall color.

The little gardens enclosed by the fence are all 25 feet square. Each one has a different color scheme, and each has a center feature with a walk. The two axes outside the Belgian fences cross in a larger circle that has a *Magnolia stellata* with *Plumbago* as a groundcover. The desired effect in these four little gardens was a blousy, cottage garden style with plants spilling over one another and even weeds being nurtured—goldenrod, violets and *Monarda* are welcome. Staking was kept to a minimum, allowing the plants to support themselves in a natural way. Every square inch of soil was to be covered

The perennial garden is the pink and blue one and includes Astilbe *'Erica', coralbells, Oriental poppies* (Papaver orientale *'Mrs. Perry')* and *Phlox paniculata 'Bright Eyes'.*

with growing plants. The selection changed from time to time as the owners learned about new varieties. The edges have undergone even more changes, because some of the edging plants (*Heuchera* for example) did not do well.

The four original gardens—fragrant, pink, blue and white hardy perennials—were a mixture of 10 to 12 different plants in the three beds of each garden (lists 1 to 4).

The cross axis leads to five steps that go down to the pool. In the area on the far side of the pool, the owners planted an interesting combination of flowering shrubs and old-fashioned roses. All of these have matured, so that eight years after planting, the shrubs give a charming enclosure for the pool.

A peony walk leads back to the house from the pool. Peonies in different varieties have been planted to extend the flowering season—early, mid and late season ('Festiva Maxima', 'Sarah Bernhardt,' 'Marie Crouse', 'Rubra Plens'). *Cimicifuga* has been planted behind the peonies for late bloom. It has been a delightful, late-blooming perennial addition. On the right of the peony walk is the tennis court and a sitting area surrounded by heaths and heathers, replaced over the years with creeping phlox and Japanese iris. (Some heaths and heathers remain, but many have not survived the

A peony walk to the tennis court is planted with a variety of peonies. Here we see 'Festiva Maxima' and 'Sara Bernhardt' with a tree lilac in the background.

hot, dry summers.) The view to the tennis court is completely hidden from the driveway by trees and flowering shrubs (list 5).

The element of surprise in a garden design adds an exciting dimension. A tour of these grounds at any season of the year gives the owners and their visitors the delightful experience of pictures changing, surprises revealed. This interesting layout and lovely planting is so much more effective than if all had been apparent at once.

PLANT LIST

LIST 1 ❦ FRAGRANT GARDEN

Aquilegia chrysantha (Columbine)

Artemisia Abrotanum (Sagebrush, mugwort)

Asclepias tuberosa (Milkweed)

Astilbe chinensis 'Pumila' (Astilbe)

Buddleia Davidii (Butterfly bush)

Dianthus plumarius 'Aqua' (Pinks)

Dianthus plumarius 'Evangeline' (Pinks)

Dictamnus albus (Gas plant)

Hemerocallis flava Thunbergii (Daylily)

Hosta grandiflora (Plantain lily)

Iris ×germanica (German iris, selected)

Iris Kaempferi (Japanese iris, selected)

Lavandula angustifolia 'Hidcote' (Lavender)

Lilium, in variety (Lilies)

Monarda didyma 'Granite Pink' (Bee balm)

Paeonia lactiflora 'Festiva Maxima' (Peony)

Philadelphus coronarius (Mock orange)

Phlox carolina 'Miss Lingard' (Phlox)

Phlox paniculata 'Dresden China' (Phlox)
Santolina virens (Santolina)
Valeriana officinalis (Garden heliotrope)

LIST 2 ✎ PINK AND BLUE

Aster Tall 'Marie Ballard' (Aster)
Astilbe Hybrid 'Erica' (Astilbe)
Centaurea montana (Mountain bluet)
Dictamnus alba 'Rubra' (Gas plant)
Heuchera sanguinea (Coralbells)
Iberis sempervirens 'Purity' (Candytuft)
Iris 'Blue Rhythm' (Iris)
Iris 'China Maid' (Iris)
Iris 'Lorilee' (Iris)
Lavandula angustifolia (Lavender)
Lilium 'Royal Aurelian' Hybrids (Lily)
Nepeta Mussinii (Catmint)
Paeonia 'Sarah Bernhardt' (Peony)
Papaver orientale 'Mrs. Perry' (Oriental poppy)
Penstemon barbatus 'Elfin Pink' (Beardtongue)
Phlox paniculata 'Bright Eyes' (Phlox)
Platycodon grandiflorus (Balloon flower)
Stokesia laevis (Stokes' aster)

LIST 3 ✎ HARDY PERENNIALS

Aconitum autumnale (Monkshood)
Anchusa myosotidiflora (Bugloss)
Anemone japonica (Anemone)
Aquilegia chrysantha (Columbine)
Aster, in variety (Aster)
Campanula carpatica (Bellflower)
Delphinium, in variety (Larkspur)
Dictamnus rubra (Gas plant)
Lilium, in variety (Lily)
Linum perenne (Flax)
Lupinus 'Russell' Hybrids (Lupine)
Papaver, in variety (Poppies)
Phlox, in variety (Phlox)
Platycodon grandiflorus (Balloon flower)
Polemonium caeruleum (Jacob's ladder)
Rudbeckia (Black-eyed Susan)
Scabiosa caucasica (Pincushion flower)
Thermopsis caroliniana (False lupine)
Veronica spicata (Speedwell)

LIST 4 ✎ WHITE

Aquilegia flabellata 'Nana Alba' (Columbine)
Arabis alpina 'Snowcap' (Rock cress)
Artemisia 'Silver King' (Mugwort)
Aster 'Mt. Ranier' (Aster)
Aster 'Snow Sprite' (Aster)
Astilbe 'White Gloria' (Astilbe)
Boltonia asteroides (Boltonia)
Campanula persicifolia 'Alba' (Bellflower)
Chrysanthemum maximum 'Victor' (Shasta daisy)
Dictamnus albus (Gas plant)
Gypsophila paniculata (Baby's breath)
Heuchera sanguinea 'White Cloud' (Coralbells)
Iberis sempervirens 'Purity' (Candytuft)
Iris, in variety (Iris; selected white)
Lilium 'Easter Parade' (Lily)
Lilium 'Silver Dream' (Lily)
Lilium 'White Majestic' (Lily)
Papaver, in variety (Poppies)
Phlox, in variety (Phlox; white)
Veronica spicata 'Icicle' (Speedwell)

LIST 5 ✎ TENNIS COURT PLANTING

Berberis Julianae (Barberry)
Cedrus atlantica 'Glauca' (Blue atlas cedar)
Crataegus Phaenopyrum (Washington hawthorn)
Cytisus scoparius (Scotch broom)
Hamamelis 'Arnold Promise' (Witch hazel)
Hamamelis mollis (Witch hazel)
Hamamelis virginiana (Witch hazel)
Hypericum calycinum 'Hidcote' (St.-John's-wort)
Juniperus chinensis 'Pfitzerana' (Juniper)
Mahonia Aquifolium (Oregon grapeholly)
Pinus Cembra (Stone pine)
Platanus × *acerifolia* (Plane tree)
Rhus Cotinus (Smoke bush)
Symplocos paniculata (Sweetleaf)
Syringa Meyeri 'Palibin' (Dwarf Korean lilac)
Tamarix 'Pink Cascade' (Tamarisk)
Thuja occidentalis 'Hetz Wintergreen' (Arborvitae)
Viburnum Carlesii (Mayflower viburnum)

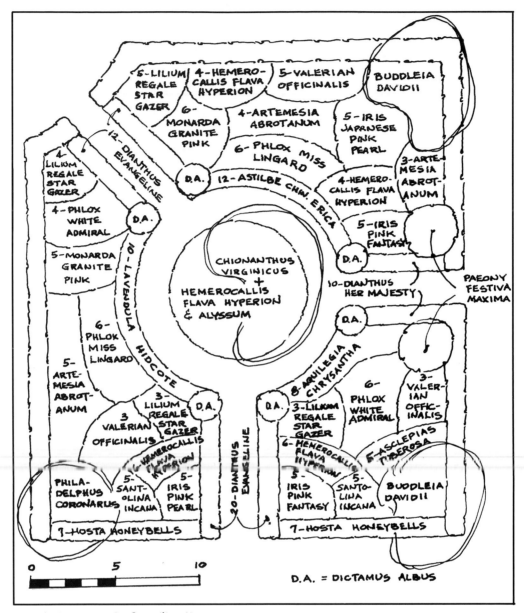

Detail: Fragrant Garden (list 1).

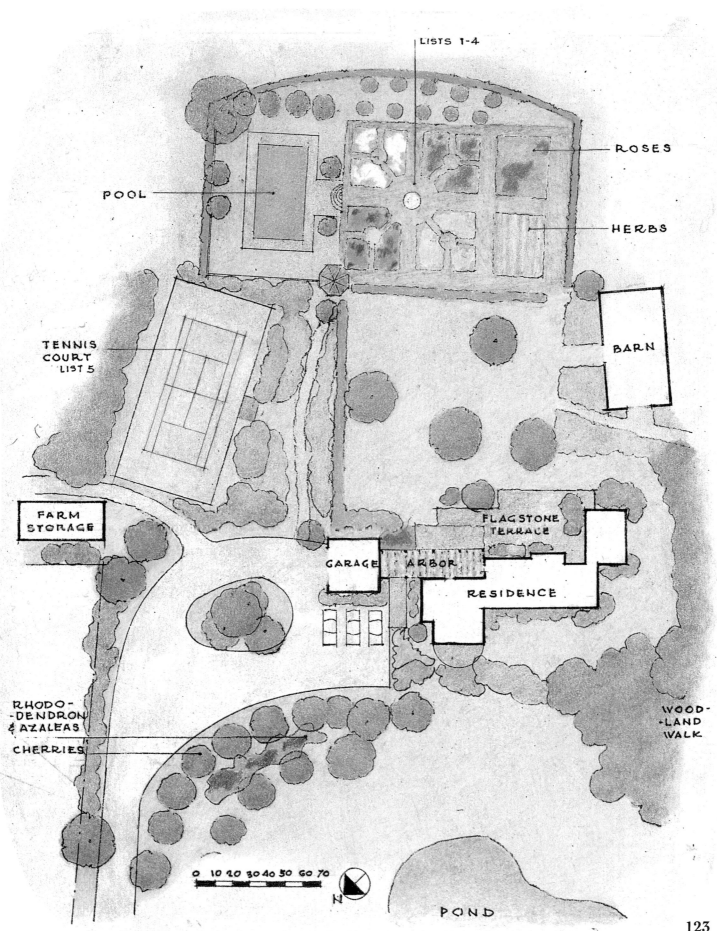

LISTS 1-4

ROSES

POOL

HERBS

TENNIS COURT LIST 5

BARN

FARM STORAGE

FLAGSTONE TERRACE

GARAGE   ARBOR

RESIDENCE

RHODO- -DENDRON & AZALEAS

CHERRIES

WOOD- LAND WALK

0 10 20 30 40 50 60 70

N

POND

123

PART VI

Some of My Favorite Plantings

This little garden with its iris, phlox, liatris, ageratum and lilies makes an excellent summer-blooming garden for a small area.

CHAPTER 15

Trees

A change in garden rooms is always possible, even the addition of a beautiful new tree if one has died or gone down in a storm. (Of course, you should review any additions on your garden plan.) Trees are becoming more and more necessary to the quality of our lives. The benefits that trees provide are numerous: shade and cooling effects in summer, windbreak and warming effects in winter, noise abatement, food production and reduced water erosion. But probably of most concern to people today is air purification, and trees can help provide this. Trees help clean the air of excess carbon dioxide emissions. It is essential to provide for trees and take care of them.

I find that some people do not think of trees as part of their garden; but in fact, trees are very important from a design standpoint. They provide structure, color, form, texture and interest—all the features you need to create an outstanding garden design. Trees are the strongest structural element in your plan—they really are the most important plant material that you will select on your site. They are a major investment as well, so it is important to select just the right ones and then to place them properly.

Trees create space. They are the roof and walls of a garden. They can be used formally in avenues or informally in groups. They attract birds and give pleasure in winter with their beautiful form and structure. Trees make effective screens, both horizontal and

This avenue of European beech trees planted 32 years ago is a pleasure to drive through in all seasons. Seen here in spring, some of the lower branches touch the ground. In fall the foliage is a clear yellow, and in winter the bare-branched form of these trees is lovely.

The crab apple recently planted at the corner of this charming old house will always stay in scale and give spring color and food for the birds. Dwarf boxwoods and myrtle complete this simple planting.

vertical; in my little, city backyard they hide the tall apartment buildings nearby. But I suppose it is in springtime, when the flowering trees break into color that people cannot fail to think of trees as an essential part of the garden. Just one fine tree can set the scale for all of your other planting. Sometimes, though, there is not even one tree to start with; this is particularly the case in new developments where contractors may have indiscriminately leveled everything to the ground. In the case of a small plot that was designed in the midst of a 100-acre hayfield there was not a single tree, so we had to plant for immediate shade. We selected a plane tree, pin oaks and several flowering crab apples and hawthorns—all fairly fast-growing. However, if you have a house set in woodland, thinning out may be all that is required. The answer may lie not in new specimens, but in high pruning of old ones for a restful, cathedral-like feeling.

Before you buy a tree, be sure you know how large it will eventually grow, and what form it will take: upright like a Lombardy poplar or cedar, oval like a sugar maple or drooping like a willow? Do you want a single- or multiple-stemmed specimen? Young plants in the nursery rarely have the shape that they will develop in 5 or 10 years. A small Chinese dogwood is as awkward as an adolescent, but in maturity it has a lovely form. Consider texture and the color of the foliage in both summer and fall. Can you look forward to rich autumn hues? Think about how trees look in winter. Some have very interesting structure and color then—for example,

This weeping beech is at the end of the garden as a focal point. Shown here in early spring before leafing-out, its twisted branches are interesting.

A multiple-stemmed gray birch is used here in this island planting for height and year-'round interest.

A cut-leaf maple is spectacular in fall and lovely throughout the year. Here it ends the perennial border.

the gray-trunked magnolias, the white birches, the red-barked Japanese maples and the shag-barked hickories.

Evergreens, usually slow-growing and therefore longer in maturing, are essential for their good, green winter color; their form; their attraction for birds—in sum, for the character they give to a planting. Conifers offer the strongest and darkest effect. When you buy young trees, branches will be full to the ground; but if you have old pines or spruces, you know how clear the trunks stand and how high the branches are above your head. White pines and hemlocks normally grow faster than other evergreens and are useful when quick screening is needed.

Set your trees so that there is room for them to develop without crowding. A 75 × 150-foot lot can accommodate just one shade tree and only two or three smaller flowering kinds. Plant the major trees with at least 30 feet between them and the smaller ones about 15 feet apart. Too many trees will soon crowd a small property. However, if you *want* to create a woodland you can follow nature's example and set trees quite close together—as close as 10 feet on center (from the stem, or center, of one tree to the stem of another).

A tree's type of root system, whether tap or fibrous, influences the spacing and also affects your choices for planting underneath. Willows, Norway maples and poplars have greedy roots close to the surface; avoid using them in lawn areas and near paving. Select one of the oaks instead, because their roots go deep into the soil, allowing a wide variety of ericaceous plants (azaleas, rhododendron and blueberries) to grow well under them. Perennial gardens can be developed under fruit trees, creating beautiful spring pictures with

A wisteria tree requires pruning, but it is delightful when in bloom. The shape is also lovely in winter.

These hemlocks form a screen with summer flowers massed in front. Ligularia with its tall, spiky yellow flowers blooms in August.

*The silver bell (*Halesia carolina*), a fast-growing tree, blooms in late May. Here by a perennial garden with a small terrace and circular bench it is a nice spot to enjoy the garden.*

the trees in flower and the early perennials blooming beneath them. Birch and crab apples are two deep-rooted, smaller trees well-suited for lawns and gardens.

As you learn to recognize trees, you will find them a never-ending source of pleasure. Driving along a parkway in winter, you will be aware of the variety of forms: the pin oak with horizontal branches, the honey locust stretching out to catch the winter light, the severely upright poplars, the graceful weeping willow that is a cloud of gold from January on. Look for the wide-spreading hawthorns with their bright red berries and the stratified sassafras growing in thickets along the edge of the road.

Guide to Tree Selection

- Choose deciduous trees in good scale for your property. Before you buy, find out about their color, texture and mature form.

- Plant evergreens as space permits.

- Check the type of root system so you will know what underplanting is feasible.

- Select trees at the nursery if at all possible and tag the best side of each tree so it can be planted to advantage on your property.

CHAPTER 16

Shade-Loving Shrubs

I am always surprised at how many people think of shrubs only as foundation plantings and don't realize how delightful they are in many places throughout the garden. I use them as specimen plants, for screening, in island plantings and for flowering-shrub borders. Some, like hydrangeas, are even fine for "picking gardens"! Whether planting in sun or shade, selecting the right plant for the right spot is often difficult. You may be overwhelmed with the variety of shrubs from which to choose. Therefore, certain things are important to consider. Before you buy a shrub, check the soil preferences (azaleas and rhododendron are acid-loving; lilacs prefer lime), leaf texture and branching characteristics. You will also want to know the height at maturity and the color of the flowers.

In this chapter I am particularly concerned with shade-loving shrubs, because a question I am often asked is "What can I plant in the shade?" You will discover that there are different kinds of shade in your garden. In areas of dappled shade, plants may receive four to five hours of filtered sunlight a day. Where shade is dense, as in thick woodland, sun may barely touch the ground. Here the soil conditions become a consideration as well. Sometimes there isn't enough soil because of the root system of surrounding trees. When this is the case, I layer 6 to 8 inches of topsoil on top of sheets of polyethylene in which holes have been punched—to allow moisture and air to reach the roots. The polyethylene prevents the roots from taking over. Given the opportunity, the roots of large trees will completely

An azalea walk can be a delightful addition to your woodland. These Exbury azaleas are blooming in late May in wonderful, rich colors.

take over any plants that you may plant beneath the tree. This new soil will provide the proper growing conditions for low-growing shrubs. Recognizing different growing conditions will help you decide what will be most suitable to plant.

You may have a house in the woods, a short path into a wooded area or just a shady area around the house on the north side. In any case, my suggestion for shrubs is fairly short. I think it best to keep to a few varieties and repeat them often. I have selected five familiar shrubs: azaleas, small-leafed rhododendron, hollies, hydrangeas and viburnums. From this group of five you can select many varieties that will grow well in different shady conditions.

Azaleas

Azaleas will bloom for nearly five months, from early April through mid-August. The earliest to bloom is the deciduous *Rhododendron mucronulatum* with a purple flower appearing before the leaves. Purple is not my favorite color, but there is a new cultivar available, 'Cornell Pink', which is lovely and lights up a spot on a hillside long before any leaves appear on the trees.

The native deciduous azaleas will bloom over a 2½-month period and, provided you give them an acid soil condition, good drainage and normal watering, the results will improve year after year. I like to use *R. Vaseyi, R. nudiflorum, R. viscosum, R. Schlippenbachii, R. molle, Azalea narcissiflora* and *R. calendulaceum.*

A. narcissiflora, a yellow fragrant azalea, grows 6 feet tall and just as wide. It blooms in late May.

R. nudiflorum, or the pinxter flower, also blooms in early spring, reaching 6 to 7 feet with small pink flowers that are slightly fragrant.

R. Schlippenbachii, the royal azalea, is one of the most beautiful azaleas. In May, just as the leaves are unfolding, large, soft pink flowers borne in clusters appear. It grows wide and is rarely taller than 10 feet.

R. Vaseyi, or pinkshell azalea, is a native azalea that has clusters of clear pink flowers before the leaves appear. In early spring it gives you an immediate lift as you see it growing at the edge of the woodland. Pinkshell azalea will reach 12 feet high and has lovely fall foliage.

R. viscosa, the swamp azalea, likes moist conditions and blooms June to July with deliciously fragrant white flowers.

134

An Azalea narcissiflora *with lovely clear yellow blossoms planted in front of a hemlock hedge.*

Pinkshell azalea (Rhododendron Vaseyi) *blossoms in May.*

R. molle, the Mollis azalea, with colors ranging from pale yellow to brilliant coppery flame color. They will grow to 6 feet and bloom well year after year in late June.

R. calendulacea is called the flame azalea. It is a native shrub, growing in the woods with pale yellow to brilliant orange flowers in late June. It grows 8 feet tall.

The recent evergreen varieties produced by Mrs. Polly Hill have added a whole new group of low-growing plants that flower in July and August. The ones I have used are 'Pink Pancake', 'Joseph Hill' (brilliant red), 'Wintergreen' (red) and 'Michael Hill' (salmon-pink).

Some azaleas are semievergreen (they lose some of their leaves in winter) and, therefore, are nice to use for their winter effect. *R. ×Hinomayo* is the best of this group because of its striking, deep red winter foliage. I would also recommend *R. kiusianum,* a low-growing white variety. *Rhododendron Satsuki* (Azalea gumpo) is a long-time favorite of mine, growing 2 feet high and 5 feet wide with pink or white flowers. It is also a favorite of rabbits, so it should be covered with chicken wire until the branches become strong.

Rhododendron

Small-leaf rhododendron are becoming more and more popular for use in gardens and around the home as they stay small, while increasing in beauty each year.

Rhododendron 'Anna Baldsiefen' grows to 2 feet with rose-colored flowers.

R. 'Dora Amateis', one of my favorites because it is so densely covered with white blossoms, reaches a height of 3 feet. (A disadvantage to this plant is that the faded blooms stay on for a long time and must be pinched off.)

Rhododendron *'Windbeam' blooms every year in this spectacular way. It is one of the best small-leaf varieties.*

R. 'Keiskei' has pale yellow flowers in spring, but needs a protected spot away from the wind.

R. 'Mary Fleming' is another yellow-blooming favorite.

R. 'Waltham' is a new variety with clear pink flowers on a 3-foot shrub.

R. 'Windbeam', my old favorite, has soft pink flowers and is very hardy. It has bloomed in my yard for 20 years. I especially enjoy picking my 'Windbeam' during the winter to use for arrangements in my house. Their pink blooms will open white when brought inside, and last three to four weeks.

If you plant these small-leaf rhododendron in a shady garden or along a walk they will always be easy to maintain as they grow very slowly and will not need much pruning. In filtered sunshine the colors of their flowers are even more attractive. Along a rocky ledge shaded by old trees that had been trimmed very high the following three newer varieties were planted and did very well:

R. 'Balta' has pale pink flowers that open to white with dark green leaves.

R. 'Laurie' has light pink flowers in May with dark green leaves.

R. 'Molly Fordham' has white flowers in May with small leathery foliage.

I have omitted the purple-flowering varieties like 'P.J.M.' and 'Purple Gem' because I feel the colors are strong and can be difficult to use unless you want an all-purple garden. The foliage, however, is extremely nice.

These small-leaf rhododendron can be used for mass plantings, particularly if you select the colors carefully. Some are very fragrant and many have lovely foliage. Often nurseries will not have these small-leaf varieties, but it is possible to find them, and they certainly will repay your search many times over with their attractive flowers.

Hollies

Hollies are divided into American, English, Chinese and Japanese species. Unlike rhododendron, whose leaves curl up in very cold weather, hollies' leaves remain green and glossy all winter long.

- The American holly, *Ilex opaca* grows well in many different locations. It is often sheared and compact and when covered with its red or yellow berries is a strong accent plant. The leaves are dark green and not very shiny.

- The English holly, *I. aquifolium* has very shiny dark green leaves. It needs a protected spot. *I. camelliaefolia* grows into a beautiful tree and is one of my favorites. One of the hardy groups is the *I. ×Meserveae* 'Blue Boy' and 'Blue Girl', a cross between *I. aquifolium* and *I. rugosa*

- The Chinese holly, *I. cornuta* has very shiny leaves. The cultivar 'Burfordii' is often used as an accent plant in a protected spot.

- The Japanese holly, *I. crenata* has many varieties. The small-leaf 'Helleri' makes an excellent low hedge; 'Convexa' grows taller and makes a good specimen plant. The *I. crenata* 'Beehive' is a very low, compact plant that really does look like a beehive.

There are also a few deciduous varieties of holly such as *I. verticillata,* and in particular the new variety 'Sparkleberry', which grows 10 feet tall and is heavy-fruiting with long-lasting berries. It is spectacular against the snow.

Hollies are among my favorite plants because they are so useful in many different places in a shady garden. You can give accent by using one of the tall-growing varieties like *I. pedunculosa,* which grows like a birch to 20 feet and has hanging clusters of red berries or a very compact, low plant like *I. crenata* 'Beehive'. Between these two heights there are hundreds of varieties and textures

*Longstalk holly (*Ilex pedunculosa*) grows like a birch tree. It holds the hanging red berries as shown here well into winter.*

from which to choose. For a shady garden I like *I. glabra, I. verticillata* and *I. ×Meserveae* 'Blue Boy' and 'Blue Girl'.

Planting hollies is possible even in the woods. In the Virginia woods I have seen them growing right up against the trunks of trees. In shady conditions a holly walk with various varieties would be fun to include on your property. Even in my little city garden I have five different varieties of hollies that grow well under the *Ailanthus* tree: *I. crenata, I. pedunculosa, I. ×Meserveae* 'Blue Princess', *I. aquifolium* and *I. crenata* 'Helleri'. Male plants are required of most varieties for berry production. Plant them within 100 feet of the female.

Hydrangeas

Hydrangeas are deciduous shrubs with a summer bloom extending from June to October. Most hydrangeas like acid soil, which ensures blue flowers. If pink flowers are desired, lime must be added to the soil. Hydrangeas are also excellent as companion plants for rhododendron, requiring the same soil conditions, but flowering at different times. Hydrangeas are free from pests and easy to grow. The foliage is rather coarse, but they are a valuable landscape plant, especially near the seashore. These plants will require space to develop so do not plant them too close together. The following varieties are ones I have used often:

Hydrangea arborescens 'Annabelle' has white flowers in June with good glossy foliage.

H. macrophylla Mariesii, 'Nikko Blue', and 'Pink & Pretty' all bloom in July.

H. paniculata 'Grandiflora,' or Peegee hydrangea, starts out with white flower clusters that turn rose-pink in the fall. It grows 20 feet tall.

H. petiolaris, or climbing hydrangea, masses itself on walls or trees with outstanding foliage, white flowers in June and interesting, exfoliating cinnamon brown bark.

H. quercifolia, or oakleaf hydrangea, has white flowers in June and July.

Hydrangea petiolaris.

Viburnum

The Viburnum family covers many varieties with good shapes and handsome foliage, flowers and fruit. Some bloom in early April, are fragrant, and easy to grow and maintain. The fruits may be red, yellow, blue or black, and are enjoyed by the birds. Some varieties such as *Viburnum* 'Lentago' have fruits that turn from green to pink to red to dark blue. The autumn foliage is usually reddish. These large-scale plants can be used as specimens, in screen plantings or in a mixed border. I have selected four that withstand shade and are easy to grow:

Viburnum Carlesii is fragrant with lovely white blossoms in early May, and I recommend it highly.

V. dilatatum 'Linden' has white blooms in June and wonderful red berries.

V. prunifolium 'Blackhaw' tolerates shade particularly well. It has white blooms in May followed by inconspicuous black fruit.

V. tomentosum, or double file viburnum, has flat white flowers in May and June, followed in July by red berries.

Behind the border of flowers, evergreens give interest with a specimen of fall-berried Viburnum tomentosum.

Viburnum tomentosum 'Shasta' has white flower clusters in June and bright red berries in the fall; it grows in a spreading horizontal manner.

Left: *The Peegee hydrangea (*Hydrangea paniculata *'Grandiflora') is a fast-grower.*

CHAPTER 17

Flowers: My Favorite Flower Combinations Month by Month

I hope those of you who already have well-established gardens may find some ideas for new additions in this chapter. Flowers are the most colorful and constantly changing part of your garden. When I think of flowers I think not only of annuals, perennials and bulbs but of flowering shrubs as well. The following are a few suggestions of plantings that I love to see in a garden.

March

For March bloom I would always include three shrubs. The first honeysuckle to bloom is *Lonicera fragrantissima,* and it has a heavenly fragrance. It is a rather rangy shrub, but delightful nonetheless. Witch hazel (*Hamamelis* ×*intermedia* 'Arnold Promise'), with spidery yellow flowers tinged with orange, will give you a lift for six to seven weeks and carry you into spring. And last, jasmine (*Jasminum nudiflorum*) is lovely with its arching yellow branches hanging over a wall. The very early bulbs for this season would include dwarf iris (*Iris verna*), only 6 inches tall, glory-of-the-snow (*Chionodoxa*) and the daffodil 'February Gold'.

Other early bulbs I like to plant in great drifts. Snowdrops (*Galanthus nivalis*) are lovely nestled among ferns in an enclosed hidden garden where they will increase each year. A collection of crocus can be used in a small lawn area. By the time the grass needs mowing they will have long finished blooming and their leaves will have died down.

The yellow yarrow and blue Nepeta *are a bright spot in this combination planting of annuals, perennials and flowering shrubs.*

Above: 'February Gold' daffodil is one of the earliest to bloom. It is a delightful bulb to use in mass plantings.

Left: 'Arnold Promise' witch hazel blooms for three to four weeks in March and early April.

April

The low-growing, 3-foot-tall forsythia 'Lynnwood Gold' adapts to garden or hillside, blooms profusely and comes back year after year. Winter aconite (*Eranthis*) is a good companion plant with this shrub, producing little yellow flowers like buttercups, about 3 inches high. This bulb self-seeds freely, and colonies are soon formed. I often plant four varieties of early daffodils: 'Minnow', 'Jenny', 'Tête-à-Tête' and 'Ice Wings'. These tiny, early daffodils really make a nice show in a small spot.

Later in April I think of the yellow-flowering dogwood, cornelian cherry (*Cornus mas*) and carpets of violets and white *Arabis*, along with grape hyacinths and daffodils, which are now out everywhere.

These daffodils bloom in late March and early April along with the yellow Fritillaria.

Early tulips are beginning to show, among them the *Tulipa Kaufmanniana*, *T. Gregii* and *T. tarda* varieties. Bergenia is an old-fashioned perennial that blooms at this time; I use it as an accent plant.

May

Of all the months in the year, May is definitely the most exciting for a gardener, with bright blue skies, warm sunny days and everything bursting into bloom. If you are looking for a new shrub or flower, and enjoy planting, this is the month for you!

You might want to consider the following shrubs, which are sometimes overlooked. They are beautiful, and can be important specimens in your garden.

Daphne × *Burkwoodii* 'Carol Mackie' is a lovely and unusual variegated shrub that was discovered and originally propagated by avid gardener Carol Mackie in her New Jersey garden. This dense, rounded, evergreen shrub reaches a height of 3 to 4 feet and is striking for the gold-banded edges of its small, rich green leaves. In May and June star-shaped, richly fragrant, pale pink flowers densely cover the shrub, making a spectacular sight. This shrub is a genetic mutation of *D.* × *Burkwoodii* 'Somerset', which has white flowers with pink edges.

Common lilacs blooming from mid-May on are usually white or purple. There are also many hybrids with lovely, rich colors like the French lilacs *Syringa* 'Ludwig Spaeth' (deep purple) and *S.* 'Katherine Havemeyer' (cobalt blue). For a stunning white lilac I like to include *S.* 'Ellen Willmott'. The fully opened, double flowers are pure white and extremely fragrant.

You can continue your lilac blooming season with the dwarf Korean lilac (*S. Meyeri* 'Palibin'), which will reach a height of only 6 feet and has lilac-pink flowers in June. The small leaves turn a copper color in the fall. *S.* 'Primrose' has a slow, wide-growing habit with soft, creamy yellow flowers. *S.* 'Sensation', on the other hand, is vigorous and narrow-growing, producing deep purple flowers with white borders. *S. villosa* becomes a small tree with light lavender, almost white flowers in late June.

The *S.* × *Prestoniae* Hybrids are a combination of two Chinese species, *S. villosa* and *S. reflexa*. They are sturdy and fast-growing, blooming about two weeks later than most French hybrids. A good example is *S.* × *Prestoniae* 'James McFarlane', growing 10 feet high with stunning pink flower heads in June.

Along this brick path lilacs and peonies are planted. Later Hypericum *will give summer bloom.*

Tulips by the base of an old plane tree make a colorful spot by the terrace in May.

All lilacs grow best in full sun with rich, well-drained alkaline soil. When they become overgrown, cut out the heavy stems, and they will bloom again.

Viburnum Carlesii, the Mayflower viburnum (also known as the Korean spice viburnum) is extremely fragrant. The masses of flowers are deep pink in bud, open pink, then mature to pure white. These blossoms are borne in 5-inch clusters, filling the air with their perfume, and are followed by black fruit.

Many other varieties of shrubs plus all the beautiful flowering trees are part of this month's burst of color, but as it's impossible to include everything, I have listed only my favorites.

For color in the beds and borders there will, of course, be tulips. I like to blend colors so that there will be groupings that harmonize. Use some of the late-blooming tulips and *Camassia,* a bulb not often planted, but with its violet-blue flowers it extends the season along with *Scilla campanulata* into June.

Among perennials to include are the bleeding hearts (*Dicentra*), very old-fashioned flowers. *D. spectabilis* grows 3 feet high with long, arching stalks; it dies back by the end of June. *D. eximia* grows 1 to 1½ feet high and will continue blooming all summer. Both come in pink and white. Also, it is nice to have a bed of lilies of the valley. I planted them under some old lilacs so that the bed covered a 20-foot area. For continuous bloom, it is wise to dig up a 1-square-foot patch every 3 or 4 years so that the roots will get better nourishment. This should be done every 5 or 6 feet.

June

June is the rose month but it is also the time for peonies, iris and many other perennials and shrubs such as mock orange (*Philadelphus*) and *Spiraea*. Mock orange is a delightful, old-fashioned shrub. My favorite, *P. coronarius*, grows 10 feet high with single white, very fragrant flowers. It will tolerate dry conditions, and is nice to use outside a bedroom window. The *Spiraea* family is again an old-fashioned group of shrubs. Many bloom in May, but the *S. japonica* cultivars in particular are excellent for June. *Spiraea* 'Little Princess' with its pink flowers will grow 3 feet tall and bloom off and on all summer; *S.* 'Alpina' has pink flowers in June and July and grows 2 feet tall.

Roses, whether in a separate garden or added in your perennial borders, are such a delight, especially now when there are many varieties that do not need spraying. If I could have only three roses I would choose 'The Fairy', a *Rosa polyantha* with pink blossoms, 'Golden Showers', a yellow climber and the hybrid tea rose 'Peace', with yellow blooms edged with pink.

Old-fashioned shrub roses are valuable for the magnificent landscape effect they give in hedging, back-of-the-border plantings

'Shot Silk', a climbing hybrid tea rose, makes a lush display of coral-pink blooms repeatedly throughout the summer on this picket fence. To the right 'Golden Wings', another repeat bloomer, adds a delicate yellow color with its single bloom. Both of these roses are fragrant.

Rosa 'Golden Wings', single yellow repeat bloomer, moderately fragrant.

or to frame a rose garden or other formal garden. They are easy to grow, require little spraying or pruning and are exceptionally hardy. I would recommend the following:

The Damask Rose
'Marie Louise'
'Mme. Hardy'
The Moss Rose
'Blanche Moreau'
'Crested Moss'
Rosa 'Betty Prior'
Rosa blanda
Rosa ×*borboniana*
'La Reine Victoria'
'Martha'
Rosa Eglanteria (sweet briar, sweet-scented foliage)
'Brenda'
'Lady Penzance'
'Lord Penzance'
Rosa Hugonis

Roses in this raised bed by a terrace bloom continually throughout the summer.

The 'Betty Prior' rose blooming here in June has repeat blooms in the fall with a darker hue.

These Siberian iris along a walk bloom well each year, but need to be divided every three years.

Lilium speciosum 'Album' has large, pure white flowers with gracefully recurving petals, making this a special lily to use in the garden.

Peonies are often used as an accent in a flower border or as a separate planting along a walk or by a fence. The old-fashioned variety 'Festiva Maxima' (white flowers with flecks of crimson, sweetly scented) is still, in my opinion, one of the best. For other varieties see chapters 10 and 14.

Iris planted in a special part of your property make a fine display. In one Connecticut property the iris garden was always on show in June and greatly admired. In another property where a lake was built, we planted many varieties around the edge.

Dwarf bearded
 'Early Sunshine'
 'Red Dandy'
Iris ensata (Kaempferi)
 'Aichi'
 'Pink Lady'
Iris Pseudacorus (Yellow flag)
Sibirica
 'Caesar'
 'Dainty Blue'
 'Super Ego'
 'White Sails'
Tall bearded
 'Blue Sapphire'
 'Jessie Viette'
 'Leonora'
 'Mulberry'

Real lilies, as opposed to daylilies, can play a very exciting part in your garden from early summer through fall. My favorites for June to July are the following:

Lilium candidum, Madonna lily
Lilium 'Connecticut Lemonglow', unspotted clear yellow
Lilium 'Enchantment', a vibrant red
Lilium 'Regale Strain', trumpet lily

July

The shrubs that bloom now are *Clethra* and *Buddleia*—the first so very fragrant and the second a great attraction for butterflies. In one of my gardens there are 10 butterfly bushes, and it is a joy to see the great variety of butterflies hovering around. Two other shrubs that are nice in the July garden are *Potentilla fruticosa* 'Primrose Beauty', with its creamy yellow flowers and spreading habit, and *Hypericum* 'Hidcote', a low-grower with large yellow blossoms.

By now many of the annuals are taking their place for color in your garden. Whether you use a one-color scheme, such as all-white, or blue and yellow, which seems to be a great favorite, there are many combinations to use. Some annuals to consider are marigolds, asters, cosmos, alyssum, zinnias, nicotiana, phlox, stock, begonias and impatiens.

The perennials this month would certainly include phlox, daylilies (*Hemerocallis*) and delphiniums; good choices for low-growing plants include astilbe, dianthus and yucca. *Yucca filamentosa*, with its swordlike foliage, grows in one corner of my garden where it is very dry. This is an old-fashioned variety, but there are several new cultivars that are interesting and wonderful for flower arrangements. Cultivated lilies for July and August bloom should include:

Lilium 'Citronella Strain', yellow and very vigorous
Lilium 'Moonlight Strain', chartreuse-yellow trumpet lilies with a lime-green reverse
Lilium 'T. Havemeyer'

This annual border with a few perennials has an edging of sweet alyssum and blue Ageratum *backed by* Phlox carolina *'Miss Lingard', cosmos,* Achillea *and* Abelia.

This white Cleome *blooms from July until frost.*

Above: *This summer flower garden at the New York Botanical Garden, divided into six separate beds for easy picking and maintenance, is filled with a variety of summer annuals.*

Above left: Buddleia *is a graceful, fast-growing shrub that needs to be cut back to 18 inches each spring in April.*

August

Buddleia will continue blooming, adding a light, airy effect to your garden. Rose of Sharon (*Hibiscus*) with its upright habit blooms for a long time. 'Lucy' (double red) and 'Diana' (single white) are two good varieties. *Caryopteris* 'Blue Mist' produces clusters of powder blue, fringed flowers until frost, and is also loved by the butterflies. The smoke bush (*Cotinus*) with its feathery, buff-colored flower panicles adds an interesting "smoky" effect in the garden. Japanese beauty-berry (*Callicarpa japonica*) is beautiful now with thousands of small lavender-pink flowers in dense cymes. The blooms are followed by spectacular violet-purple berries, which often last until Christmas.

Along with the flowering shrubs, summer bulbs (*Gladiolus*), perennials (*Veronica* and *Hosta*) and annuals (zinnias, cleomes, dahlias

A small shady perennial border shows li-lacs, phlox, Lythrum and dahlias with an edging of Vinca and pink begonias.

A corner of a summer flower garden show-ing dahlias, Phlox paniculata 'Bright Eyes', blue Ageratum and Cleome.

and ageratums) make colorful and interesting combinations in your garden. Cultivated lilies blooming from August to September include:

Lilium auratum platyphyllum, lily of Japan, white with golden streaks and spotted with crimson

Lilium 'Oriental Mixture', a range of colors and very fragrant

Lilium speciosum 'Rubrum', pendant flowers white with crimson and very fragrant

September

After Labor Day a flower garden takes on a new look. With the cooler nights it seems that many flowers have a brighter color. Certainly many of the annuals bear this out.

The fall-blooming chaste tree (*Vitex Agnus-castas* 'Latifolia') has feathery gray foliage with lavender-blue flowers—a beautiful plant at this time of year.

Shady places can have Japanese anemones (pink and white anemones and the silver-gray artemisia do well together), while a very sunny area can include Montauk daisies and *Sedum spectabile* 'Autumn Joy'.

Don't forget the fall-blooming crocus (*Crocus speciosus*) and colchicums. These large crocuslike flowers are a valuable addition to the fall garden. In spring colchicums produce coarse leaves that die

Japanese anemones in various colors are excellent for fall-blooming shady spots.

Colchicum 'Lilac Wonder', a fall-blooming crocus, can be planted in late August and it will bloom in the fall.

back in June; then the flowers appear in early fall on 10- to 12-inch stems, without evidence of any leaves at all. Plant colchicums in a groundcover of ivy or pachysandra. This groundcover will camouflage the ripening foliage of the colchicums. Like fall crocus, colchicums are best planted in late summer.

October

In October many of the flowering shrubs, such as *Pyracantha* and several species of viburnums, will have vivid fall berries that are spectacular to see and enjoyed by the birds. Certain early-blooming perennials will put forth a few flowers at this time; these include *Delphinium* and *Phlox carolina* 'Miss Lingard'. Chrysanthemums in all their magnificent variety are at their peak now. And don't forget "the last rose of summer." Many roses are blooming now. In fact, with proper planning you can expect to have flowers until the first frost—and often beyond!

Some Final Thoughts

Over a long career, I have seen many changes in what people want for their gardens. I recall when clients asked that their perennial gardens be given up and unusual evergreens be substituted; when wildflowers, which were at first placed here and there in lawns and fields, were grouped together along the edge of an open lawn for a neater look; when vegetables were so popular that front lawns were plowed up for a little patch of organically grown vegetables (enclosed, of course, by a fence to keep the rabbits and dogs out). However, the one thing that has withstood the test of time is the idea of having a series of garden rooms—self-enclosed areas each with a different emphasis so that as you wander around a property, be it large or small (chapters 14 and 3, for example), there is always something of interest.

It is always a challenge to walk around a new site and examine the existing conditions (especially if the site is unusual and offers various solutions), to listen to a client's ideas, to find out what is wanted and then to develop a solution that is practical and beautiful and fulfills their dreams. This is the most rewarding part of my career. Sometimes the solutions are far from obvious, having less to do with plantings and design than one might think. For example, on one small property with a very large house, there was little space for designing gardens. Selecting the colors of the furniture on a wide summer porch and relating this to the small lawn area and shrub border made the whole place seem larger.

The sound of water adds a certain cooling quality to the air, so I have included a water feature in many of my gardens. I have been fortunate to have had a wonderful company, Rockwater, build many features small and large, each one quite different—from the 30-foot drop waterfall in chapter 8 to the elegant water table overflow on a large Georgian terrace in chapter 13.

Many people ask for a garden filled with flowers from early spring to late fall, very low maintenance and all within a limited budget. This is impossible! However, I do hope you have picked up suggestions from the preceding chapters that can be adjusted to suit your own ideas and your own site and that will help provide you with the garden you want. Let me summarize some of my thoughts regarding planning and planting.

- Decide how you want your property developed. Some people like to have a neat look at all times, others like to have things growing all over each other. Are your garden rooms to be formal or informal?

- How much time and money do you want to spend on development and maintenance? If maintenance must be limited, then don't plan too many gardens. If your house is a year-'round home, the emphasis should be on interesting evergreens, as well as color throughout the year. If it is just a summer home, then only the summer months need to be considered.

- When to plant—spring or fall? There are advantages to spring planting if your site is ready, for then you have the whole season to enjoy your landscaping. However, on some sites construction— the leveling of a grade or building of a sitting wall, terrace or patio—is delayed so that spring planting has to be postponed. Planting in summer is difficult as extra watering is necessary, and without this plants can dry out quickly. (However, I would like to caution against indiscriminate watering. In these environmentally sensitive times, water conservation is important to consider.) Fall planting is ideal as there is usually moisture in the ground and the earth is very workable. Evergreens should be planted by November 1. Deciduous plants can be planted until the ground freezes. (*Note:* Keep all plants well watered until the ground freezes.)

- Gardens are always changing. What is neat and trim the first year can become overgrown and frowzy the next. You don't plant "forever," so be ruthless sometimes. Give an unwanted plant to someone else.

- Take care of your plants with water and fertilizer.

• Keep a notebook of what you plant and when. Note the botanical names.

• It is wise to note the vagaries of weather. There was a rainy fall in 1989 and a bitter cold December. Trees and shrubs never had an opportunity to accustom themselves gradually to the cold and many died. This can happen from time to time, but there is nothing you can do to prevent it.

• Get the best nursery available to help you. A knowledgeable nurseryman can be of service for years.

Gardens are a luxury, but what you obtain is a satisfaction far beyond the dollars and cents involved. I think of a peony that my grandfather planted nearly 75 years ago. Then it cost 15 cents—a large amount for a small plant in those days. It has bloomed every year. I look forward to the big, beautiful blooms each June, but I know that if I can't see them, they will still be beautiful. So last, I would say: Enjoy your garden and share with others your knowledge, your plants and the joy of gardening.

APPENDIX

Plant Societies

The American Horticultural Society
7931 East Boulevard Drive
Alexandria, Virginia 22308

The American Rhododendron Society
14635 Southwest Bull Mountain Road
Tigard, Oregon 97223

The American Rose Society
P. O. Box 30,000
Shreveport, Louisiana 71130

Holly Society of America
407 Fountain Green Road
Bel Air, Maryland 21014

Botanic Gardens

Arnold Arboretum of Harvard
  University
125 Arborway
Jamaica Plain, Massachusetts 02130
(617) 524–1718

Brooklyn Botanic Garden
1000 Washington Avenue
Brooklyn, New York 11225
(718) 622-4433

Clark Botanic Garden
193 I.U. Willets Road (off Glen Cove
  Road)
Albertson, New York
(516) 621-7568

New York Botanical Garden
Southern Boulevard and 200th Street
Bronx, New York 10458
(212) 220–8700

Planting Fields Arboretum
Planting Fields Road
Oyster Bay, New York 11771
(516) 922–0479

Wave Hill
675 West 252nd Street
Bronx, New York 10471
(212) 549–2055

Landscape Contractors and Nurseries

The Bayberry Nursery
Amagansett, New York 11930
(516) 267-3000
Trees, shrubs, perennials

Carlson's Gardens
Box 305
South Salem, New York 10590
(914) 763–5958
Azaleas, rhododendron, small-leafed
  rhododendron

Di Stefano Landscaping, Inc.
1056 Northern Boulevard
Roslyn, New York 11576
(516) 627–3524

Environmentals
Mr. James Cross
Box 730
Cutchogue, New York 11935
(516) 734–6439
Wholesale — unusual plants, pot-grown
  shrubs, trees

Frankenbach's Deerfield Nursery, Inc.
Mr. Michael Graham
Deerfield Road
P. O. Box 624
Water Mill, New York 11976
(516) 283–0785

Henry Feil and Son
25 Prospect Avenue
Hewlett, New York
(516) 599–1985
Unusual plants

Hicks Nurseries, Inc.
Between Post and Ellison Avenues
Jericho Turnpike
Westbury, New York 11590
(516) 334–0066

Hillside Gardens
Mr. Frederick McGourty
P. O. Box 641
515 Litchfield Road
Norwalk, Connecticut 06058
(203) 542-5345
Perennials

Kale Landscape Nursery
133 Carter Road
Princeton, New Jersey 08540
(609) 921-9248

Keil Brothers Nursery
220-15 Horace Harding Boulevard
Bayside, New York 11364
(718) 229-5042

Klehm Nursery
Route 5, Box 197
South Barrington, Illinois 60010
(312) 551-3715
Perennials, especially iris and peonies

L & M Landscaping
P. O. Box 1945
Easthampton, New York 11937
(516) 324-9408

Miller Brothers, Inc.
Mr. David M. Purshall
379 Glen Cove/Greenvale Highway
Greenvale, New York 11548
(516) 676-6221

Oliver Nurseries
1159 Bronson Road
Fairfield, Connecticut 06430
(203) 259-5609
Rhododendron, azaleas, evergreens,
   rock plants

Donald F. Pollitt, Inc.
100 Jericho Turnpike
Westbury, New York 11590
(516) 997-3777

Rockwater Ltd.
P. O. Box 882
Amagansett, New York 11930
(516) 267-7573
Construction of ponds and waterfalls

Rosedale Nurseries
51 Saw Mill River Road
Hawthorne, New York 10532
(914) 769-1300

Roslyn Nursery
211 Burrs Lane
Dix Hills, New York 11746
(516) 643-9347
Rhododendron and azaleas

S. Scherer & Sons
104 Waterside Avenue
Northport, New York 11768
(516) 261-7432
Water plants

Shelter Island Nursery
P. O. Box 479
St. Mary's Road
Shelter Island, New York 11964
(516) 749-0490

Sprainbrook Nursery, Inc.
448 Underhill Road
Scarsdale, New York 10583
(914) 723-2382

Terra Care
P. O. Box 90
Malden, West Virginia 25306
(304) 925-4754

Andre Viette Farm and Nursery
Route 1, Box 16
Fisherville, Virginia 22939
(708) 943-2315
Perennials

Weston Nurseries, Inc.
E. Main Street (Route 135)
P. O. Box 186
Hopkinton, Massachusetts 01748-0186
(617) 435-3414
Trees, shrubs, perennials

Galen Williams
27A Spring Close Highway
Easthampton, New York 11937
(516) 324-6220
Unusual plants and planting

INDEX